Instructor's Guide
with Test Items

COMMUNICATION IN ACTION:
TEACHING THE LANGUAGE ARTS
Fourth Edition

DOROTHY GRANT HENNINGS
Kean College of New Jersey

"Will you walk a little faster?" said a whiting to a snail,
"There's a porpoise close behind us, and he's treading on my tail.
See how eagerly the lobsters and the turtles all advance!
They are waiting on the shingle--will you come and join the dance?
    Will you, won't you, will you, won't you, will you join the dance?
    Will you, won't you, will you, won't you, won't you join the dance?

from Lewis Carroll's <u>Alice in Wonderland</u>

HOUGHTON MIFFLIN COMPANY   BOSTON
        Dallas   Geneva, Illinois
      Palo Alto   Princeton, New Jersey

to the classroom teachers who shared their ideas and materials with me and who tried the idea in their classrooms

Printed in the U.S.A.
ISBN: 0-395-52669-8
ABCDEFGHIJ-BW-96543210

CONTENTS

PREFACE

I. BASIC ASSUMPTIONS

Three assumptions are inherent in the design of the fourth edition of
Communication in Action and this accompanying instructor's guide.

A. What Is to Be Learned

The first assumption bears upon the learnings to be acquired through a college-
level course in the language arts. At completion, the pre- or in-service
teacher should be able to state the following with some degree of confidence:

I feel comfortable with language teaching strategies that are different
from the more traditional approaches I experienced as a student in elementary
schools.

I know a variety of teaching strategies for developing language learning.
I can integrate these strategies into content-area sequences that meet a broad
range of individual language needs. I enjoy experimenting with new ideas and
figuring out original ways to do things.

I know a variety of forms of creative expression--for example, haiku,
finger play, personification, squiggling. I can create using these forms and
take delight in the process of creating.

I am familiar with many children's books that can serve as bases for
language experience and that stimulate children to read. I enjoy reading and
sharing literature with children.

I enjoy language, especially playing with sounds, words, and meanings in
creative ways.

I can analyze language learning sequences. I can identify the language
goals to be achieved, the assumptions underlying actions, and the purposes for
which specific teaching strategies are being employed.

I can organize an elementary classroom using a combination of personalized,
small group, and total class activities to meet the differing needs of all the
children.

I can use textbooks and technology creatively in a lesson.

I am (or will be) a dynamic teacher of the language arts.

These learnings are intentionally not expressed in strict behavioral or
performance terms. Some fundamental goals, such as taking delight in the
process of creating and enjoying experimentation with new ideas, are clearly
appreciations, beyond objective and immediate measurement. Ultimately it is
the teacher or teacher-in-the-making who must evaluate his or her own growth
towards these goals, with actual success in teaching being the sought-for
result.

B.   How Learnings Are Acquired

To achieve these learnings, college students of the language arts must have
firsthand encounters with instructional strategies, language, and literature,
in addition to reading and talking about them. It is a truism that must of us
feel comfortable with and do what we know most intimately. Therefore,
instruction must permit pre-and in-service teachers complete and direct
involvement in dynamic processes of learning and teaching language. Complete
and direct means that teachers must actually be part of classroom sessions in
which they themselves cooperatively compose stories and poems, edit what they
have written, reconstruct stories from story cards, orchestrate a choral
speaking or finger play, brainstorm, clarify values together, experience with
all the senses, build words out of units of meaning, and create mind-stretching
hyperboles, similes, and metaphors. They need to have the experience of
learning in learning stations, of "languaging" in small groups, of reporting to
the class, of listening for specific purposes, of reading for other purposes,
of working independently on projects related to their own needs. Those who
have fully experienced these components of language instruction are more likely
to apply them in their own teaching.

     The application of dynamic teaching strategies to real classrooms obviously
is a part of building and refining skill. In this respect, there must be some
opportunity in elementary classrooms for teachers to try out and experiment
with ideas encountered in college sessions and readings.

C.   Relationship between Action and Theory

A third assumption underlying this book is that theory is most meaningfully
developed by working from specific ideas about teaching and learning. Theory
is the sum of all the conceptions and assumptions that underlie what teachers
do in classrooms. Pre-and in-service teachers learn theory by experiencing
productive language and instructional strategies in college-course sessions, by
applying them in elementary classrooms, by examining underlying assumptions,
and by generalizing from specific instances that they have encountered firsthand. This is inductive teaching, and it is more meaningful than learning
lists of theoretical precepts set forth in lectures or texts.

D.   The Design of Communication in Action and The Instructor's Guide

Assumptions about the purposes of language arts method for teachers, the means
to attain these ends, and the place of theory in teaching have influenced the
direction of this guide. Ideas for structuring creative encounters with
language and with instructional strategies and pre- and in-service teachers are
a major component of this guide.

     In addition, detailed descriptions of actual elementary language arts
experiences are found within each chapter of Communication in Action, fourth
edition. These vignettes extend teachers' awareness of the potential of
various teaching-learning strategies and provide a sense of you-are-there-
looking-over-the-teacher's-shoulder-in-the-classrooms. They also provide case-
study material for analysis in college methods or in-service courses--material
that teachers can look at closely to develop in-depth understanding of
teaching-learning strategies. Through analysis, pre-and in-service teachers
can attain a heightened conception of the nature of language arts goals, of the
assumptions underlying instruction, of ways to achieve these goals, and of ways
of planning for innovative instruction. These descriptions as well as the

firsthand "languaging" pre- and in-service teachers experience within the methods class serve as preliminary models for creating similarly structured sequences with children and for inductively developing a theory of language arts instruction.

II.   HOW THIS GUIDE IS STRUCTURED

Each chapter of this guide parallels a chapter in the fourth edition of Communication in Action and offers activities that complement themes developed in the text.   Each chapter provides:

A.   A brief overview that presents major themes of the text chapter.

B.   A statement of learnings, or goals, to be developed through reading the test and completing the activities at the end of each section.   These may be duplicated and given to course participants as a self-analysis guide.

C.   Questions to be used with the teaching-in-action vignettes.   These can be a beginning for class discussion.

D.   Ideas for creative encounters with language and with instructional strategies.   Ideas includes ways to structure analytical sessions, formats for languaging together, topics for individual reporting, and films for classroom viewing and analyzing.   Again, this material can be duplicated for use in course sessions.

E.   Examination questions, including short discussion and multiple-choice items.   Obviously, the multiple-choice questions offer a limited measure of the objectives of a language arts methods course, for it is impossible to determine through them whether a teacher or teacher-to-be can design, create, rank-order, identify assumptions, enjoy, delight, or take pleasure.   These items are useful only when an instructor desires an objective indicator that participants have studied the text.   In this respect, they are most helpful in reference to the background-information chapters--Chapters One, Two, Three and Twelve--and the informational content of the other chapters.   More helpful are the short discussion questions that ask teachers to perform functions associated with teaching.   Since more of these problemlike questions are supplied than are needed for the purposes of evaluation, some can be used as a basis for group and class problem solving.   In addition, at the end of this guide are essay-type midterm and final examinations that assess future teachers' ability to analyze, plan and organize.

F.   Masters, that can be converted into transparencies and projected and/or can be reproduced and distributed to students.   These masters can be the basis of class sessions.

III.   USING COMMUNICATION IN ACTION

Communication in Action and this companion guide can be used in diverse teaching-learning situations:

A.   In field-based and/or competency-based courses and workshops.   For teachers studying language arts instruction as part of field-based and/or competency-based courses or as part of in-service workshops, the book provides the framework for individual study and seminar-type sessions.   In such instances, early in the course, teachers should quickly read through the text.   Based on their initial reading, teachers develop what might be called <u>The Plan</u>--specific teaching strategies they will try out in their elementary classrooms.

To facilitate development of <u>The Plan</u>, you may wish to duplicate and distribute the list of general learnings found on the opening pages of this manual and perhaps the list of learnings at the start of each chapter. Draw attention to the sections in the text entitled "Building and Refining Your Teaching Skills." Pre- and inservice teachers select from among these activities and create additional personalized activities they believe will help them reach stated goals. Activities chosen and devised are tried out and evaluated in ongoing classroom lessons with elementary children.

In such courses, early seminar sessions in which the college instructor and teachers participate are times for experiencing language and innovative instructional strategies. The college instructor leads seminar students in creative work with language and teaching and develops among students a sense of confidence and know-how about strategies they may have never seen in action. This is important when teachers are functioning in traditional settings where few creative and innovative methods are already in practice. Early seminar sessions are the time and place to use "Ideas for Creative Encounters with Language and with Instructional Strategies."

During later seminar sessions, practicing teachers and teacher-interns can report on language experiences they have shared with children. They can describe their preliminary plans, point out their most and least successful strategies, identify assumptions underlying their approach, and display some physical evidence of what went on. Evidence can take the form of children's composition work or experience charts, video- or audio tapes of classroom sessions, materials used during a lesson, or comments by an observer. During final seminar sessions, teachers and teacher-interns can project their own theories of language instruction--what they feel makes good instruction and why.

Throughout the course, practicing teachers will need guidance from the college instructor. Especially as students prepare <u>The Plan</u> and make choices as to which teaching-skill-building activities to attempt, they will want to talk about their uncertainties. As they proceed to design language-learning experiences and as they adapt ideas from <u>Communication in Action</u> for use in their own classrooms, they may also require personalized assistance. Hence, in field-based courses and in-service workshops, the individual conference becomes a time for identifying personalized goals and for ironing out individual problems. This is true at both the graduate and undergraduate levels.

B. In campus-based courses and workshops. Where teachers and teachers-to-be are studying language arts methods as part of regularly scheduled campus-based courses, <u>Communication in Action</u> and this guide are equally applicable. Over seventy suggestions for college-level sessions of a nonlecture variety are detailed. Most require active involvement with teaching processes and the analysis of those processes. More than 60 masters are included. These can be made into transparencies to be projected during class sessions and/or duplicated and distributed to students to guide reading and discussion. Also many topics for individual and group reporting that complement the content of the textbook chapters are presented. Placed on task cards, these topics can be chosen by course participants to be presented at an appropriate point in the course. In addition, there are question sequences to accompany the teaching-in-action segments that can provide discussion starters and, in some instances, suggestions for using the Forums. Since most graduate and undergraduate courses consist of about 30 to 36 one-hour sessions or 15 to 16 two-and-a-half-hour sessions, the instructor can structure a considerable portion of a course around these suggestions, supplemented, of course, with lectures and sessions of his or her own creation.

Appendix A supplies two syllabuses for campus-based language arts courses, each structured around a different time pattern. These syllabuses can be adjusted to meet the exigencies of particular college teaching situations.

The syllabuses as well as the suggested activities have been tried by the writer in both graduate and undergraduate courses in the language arts and in workshops given for teachers in school districts. Many of the examples of classroom activities detailed in the text, as well as the samples of children's creative expression, have been contributed by teachers who experienced language arts instructional strategies directly in graduate or undergraduate courses or workshops. Although you are asked to provide comments at the end of this guide, the writer would also appreciate hearing comments about the successes and problems encountered as you apply ideas. Kindly send ideas, suggestions, and samples to:

Dr. Dorothy Grant Hennings
Professor of Language Arts Education
Kean College of New Jersey
Union, New Jersey 07083
(201) 527-2175

INTRODUCTION: GETTING STARTED

I. PREFACE THEME--WHAT IS INTENDED

The preface introduces readers to the overarching philosophy of <u>Communication in Action</u> and its organization.

II. PREFACE GOALS--WHAT IS TO BE LEARNED

Having read the preface and completed a preview survey of the book, the prospective or in-service teacher should be able to state:

   I know the value of activating prior knowledge before reading on a topic and the value of predicting before reading.

   I know how to survey a text before reading it, using the preface, the table of contents, and the features of the book.

III. IDEAS FOR CREATIVE ENCOUNTERS WITH LANGUAGE AND WITH INSTRUCTIONAL
      STRATEGIES

A. Mapping Prior Knowledge

Using the title web on the opening page of the preface, ask students to brainstorm their present thoughts and feelings about language arts. As students suggest points, have them record the points above the title web. You record the points on a transparency (see Preface Master 1) or a chalkboard web similar to the one in the book. Also ask students: What do you hope to learn through a course in language arts, or language arts and reading? Record suggestions on the web to show their interrelationships.

B. Surveying the Preface

Encourage students to survey the preface by reading the first paragraph and the section entitled "An Invitation to the Dance." Ask students to survey the subheads--for example, "Audience and Purpose," "Revisions in This Edition," and "Organization and Features." Ask them to write, based on each heading, a question they hope to answer from reading that subsection of the preface. Using the Preface, Master 1, or chalkboard web, model the writing of questions and add those questions below the web. Then have students read the preface to answer their questions. Ask: What do you hope to learn through reading

1

from the preface. Ask: How is Communication in Action organized? What features are integral parts of the book? Suggest that students turn to each part opener and read the chapter summaries found there. Ask: What is the focus of each part? What does this organization say about teaching language arts, and what can you anticipate learning from the textbook?

2. Ask students to select any one chapter to survey. Using whatever chapter they select, ask: How does the chapter open? Why do you think the author began the chapter in this way? (Talk at this point about the purpose of prereading/webbing prior ideas and of writing questions, based on the subheadings, to be answered through the reading.) Ask: What does the author do next in the chapter? What do you think is the author's purpose in describing classroom interaction in this way? (Talk about the Teaching-in-Action vignettes.) Ask: What is the system of headings and subheadings within a chapter? What guidance does this system give you as you read? Have students survey the figures. Ask: What kind of information do the figures give you? Draw attention to the margin notes, and ask: What kind of information do the margin notes supply? Flip to a Forum box, and ask: What is to be the purpose of these featured boxes? How should you use them in studying? With students, turn to the end of the chapter. Ask: What is the purpose of this summary? How should you use this section in reading the text? (Point out that some students find it helpful to read the summary section of any textbook chapter before reading the chapter.) Draw students' attention to the related readings, the references, and how those references are identified in the text.

3. Tell students that when you open a textbook, you look it over, or survey it, before reading it. Ask students to review the steps to take in surveying a textbook. (A student scribe might record those steps on the chalkboard.)

4. Ask: When working with children, how can you use what we have just done as part of a content-area language arts and reading activity? How can you use a preview survey of this kind in your own teaching?

D. Continuing Activities: The College Language Arts Classroom as a Model of the Ongoing Elementary Language Arts Classroom

College students of the language arts learn much about bringing communication into action by doing some of the same things they will lead young children in doing. You have already seen examples of this hands-on, or "modeling," approach to the teaching of language arts in sections A, B, and C, of this introduction. In addition, from the first class session onward through the term, involve students in continuing activities (e.g., read-alouds and dialogue journals) just the way you would an elementary class.

1. Read-alouds. At the beginning of each session, read aloud to the class a portion of a children's book, preferably one that you would share with an upper-elementary group, since college students often assume that reading aloud is a strategy application only in lower grades. For that purpose, use an "emotionally grabbing" book with short chapters. This author has successfully used Sarah Plain and Tall by Patricia MacLachlan (Harper & Row, 1985). Read it aloud, chapter by chapter, day by day, following the Directed Reading-Thinking Activity/Directed Listening-Thinking Activity (DRTA/DLTA) format of predicting, listening to verify predictions, and discussing predictions that is modeled in the lesson plan in Chapter 1, Figure 1.7. The lesson plan in Chapter 1, which

2

is intended for use with Chapter 1 of <u>Sarah, Plain and Tall</u>, emphasizes characterization. With Chapter 2 of <u>Sarah</u>, you can read and followup with a cooperatively written letter to Sarah, to introduce letter writing. With Chapter 3 of <u>Sarah</u>, you can emphasize setting--comparing and contrasting Maine and the setting somewhere on the plains. Ask students to create a chart for recording differences. Ask them to hypothesize, based on story clues, exactly where on the plains the story is set. Encourage students, in groups, to plan read-aloud for the successive chapters. Have volunteers do their read-alouds for the class, just as they would with a fourth- or fifth-grade class.

For third- or fourth-grade read-alouds, other good books you may want to use with college students in teacher-education programs are Sid Fleischman's <u>The Whipping Boy</u> (Greenwillow, 1986), Joanne Henry's <u>Log Cabin in the Woods</u> (Macmillan, 1988), and Fleischman's <u>McBroom's Ear</u> (Little, Brown, 1982) or any of his other McBroom books. Read one of these books aloud with students, chapter by chapter, over the course of a semester.

2. <u>Dialogue journals</u>. Starting, too, from the first or second session of the course, have students use the first five or so minutes to write in their dialogue journals. To get them started on the first day, ask them to introduce themselves to you in their first entry. And, of course, you should write an introduction about yourself in your journal as students write in theirs. Share your entry by sitting in the Author's Chair or Sharing Place, whichever you prefer to call that spot where students and teacher will share their writings during the semester. After you have read your entry, ask students whether they have any questions about you that were not covered in your entry. When you have finished sharing, ask for one or two volunteers to share their entries and to elaborate, based on others' questions.

Using the dialogue journals, you must reply to students' entries, writing a brief response, asking questions, or commenting on content, but not correcting errors. Journals are places for encouraging writing and communication.

Because few colleges have hardcover "copybooks" to use as journals, this author has used blue books (exam booklets). On the first day, students cross out the words <u>Examination Booklet</u>, and in large letters write <u>MY WRITING JOURNAL</u>. They put their names and addresses on the cover in lieu of the typical index card of information requested in many classes. College students seem to enjoy "talking to" the instructor and getting to know her through this medium of communication. Typically, students write about once a week in their journals. Here are a few sample unedited entries written by one student (and reprinted with her permission) in an undergraduate certification program, with the instructor's replies shown in handwritten form.

INTRODUCTION

Dear Dr. Hennings,

First of all, this has not been a great day for me.
My car broke down; I had to "hitch" a ride to class. I
feel just miserable now.

However, with minor inconveniences such as I have
described, I know that I am a very blessed person. I have
my health, three wonderful sons, a kind and supportive
husband.

Sometimes I try to focus on those less fortunate and
my "disasters" are trivial in respect to theirs.

As I write I feel myself calming down. (This was a
wonderful idea and at such an appropriate time <u>for me</u>.)

I am one of Kean College's <u>older</u> students and I want
desperately to teach school. I think I'm almost there!

Thank you for the opportunity to express my "stress"
in writing.

Cheri Philips, February 9

We all have those days!

Exactly ... if you have that / you / are blessed.

How old are your sons?

Yes

Writing can serve the same / with children.

Dear Dr. Hennings,

I was very concerned with my paper for you tonight. I
tried my best and gave it 100% of me. As always in doing
a paper for an instructor for the first time, I am rather
uncertain as to what each one really wants.

I also found that I didn't do any reading for this
class (I'm sorry). Since I am carrying nine (9) credits
in the evening, I have to distribute my limited time
between all three courses.

Thank you for your kind words. I did have a better
day. Also, to answer your questions, my sons are 17, 13,
and 9 (not to mention my husband).

Journal writing is wonderful!

Cheri Philips, Feb. 16

That is a full night load. You will have to budget your time carefully.

You do not look more than 30. I would never have realized you could have a 17-year old.

How are you doing on your oral presentation?

2/23/88

As time draws nearer, I grow very nervous in
anticipation of giving my oral presentation.

I don't appear shy, but I am. I find that I do well
in a group of children. Sometimes I feel as if my peers
are judging me. I would like to overcome this. Any
suggestions from a professional?

Cheri

As a younger person I was shy too. I / forced / myself to / present.

Now I love it. You will also.

Practice ... be well prepared Select something / with considerable / repetition Involve the class.

/88

The anticipation is over. I was quite nervous even though I made my family listen to my story over and over again. My homemade animals will be added to my library material.

I'm glad I did the presentation and I'm glad I got to see other stories done in unusual ways. I'm sure I will remember some of the great ideas for future use.

C

And you did a fine job.

You looked so happy after you presented.

CHAPTER 1

TEACHING FOR COMMUNICATION--A NATURAL APPROACH
TO THE LANGUAGE ARTS

I. CHAPTER THEMES--WHAT IS INTENDED

Chapter 1 introduces readers to a language arts program in which oral- and
written-language experiences blend and oral-language activities are a thread in
reading and writing activity. It describes ways to structure language
activities based on firsthand, literature, and content-area experiences and way
to organize language-play sessions. The chapter explains how to use large-
group, small-group, and independent learning to achieve language goals,
outlines steps in lesson planning, and suggests ways to use reading series,
textbooks, and technological aids, including computers.

II. CHAPTER GOALS--WHAT IS TO BE LEARNED

Having read the chapter and completed the skill-building activities, one should
be able to state:

    I can explain four general beliefs about language arts instruction.

    I can explain the rationale for oral-language activities as the thread in
language lessons.

    I can describe ways to build language lessons based on firsthand
experiences, literature experiences, content-area study, and language play.

    I can write a lesson plan that includes objectives, activities, materials,
and evaluation.

III. IDEAS FOR CREATIVE ENCOUNTERS WITH LANGUAGE AND WITH INSTRUCTIONAL
     STRATEGIES

A. Survey of Chapter 1

Ask students to brainstorm ideas that come to mind relative to the chapter
title and to record those ideas above the title web on the first page of the
chapter. Encourage students to survey the chapter headings and the summary
paragraph at the end of the chapter and to write questions or predictions to
guide their reading. Have them write these items beneath the title web from
lines attached to it. Remind students that in college texts there is often
space around the title where they can record "Getting Ready to Read" notes.
Tell them that they can use a similar "Getting Ready to Read" strategy as
children prepare to read a selection from a content-area textbook, except that

youngsters create their prereading webs on paper, not in their books. Use Chapter 1, Master 1 to guide the prereading study when pursued as a class activity, and record brainstormed ideas on the Master as students write their notes in their books.

B. Discussion of Beliefs about Language Arts Instruction

Use Chapter 1, Master 2 as the basis for a discussion in which students summarize the beliefs about language arts instruction given in Chapter 1. As students review each of the beliefs from the text, a student can serve as scribe and record points directly on the projected transparency. Then guide students to talk about what each belief means in terms of what they will be doing as they teach language arts--the kinds of activities they will use, the ways they will structure lessons, and so forth. Guide the discussion into consideration of advantages and disadvantages, as well as comparisons with what students see occurring in some classrooms.

C. An Integrated Language Arts Session Based on a Storybook

Early in a language arts methods course, pre- and in-service teachers should be part of an integrated, literature-based language experience. Here is the design for such an experience. Through it, college students become aware of innovative teaching strategies.

1. Read aloud the picture storybook The Girl Who Loved Wild Horses by Paul Goble (Bradbury, 1978). Ask students to listen for words that describe wild horses. Share the pictures as you go along, just as you would with a group of youngsters. As you read, you may wish to play a musical recording as background accompaniment to establish a mood.

2. At the end of the story listening, ask students to offer wild-horse words-- brainstorming style--giving words they remember from the story and any others that come to mind. Record these words on charting paper. As students announce difficult words, have one student, serving as Dictionary Sleuth, check the spellings and/or meanings.

3. Guide students in composing a short nature thought. Start by recording the word horse, centered on an upper line of a second piece of charting paper. Ask students to suggest a second line of adjectives that describe the horse but do not end in the suffix -ing. As a group, students should try out various arrangements of words, searching with your creative guidance for an arrangement that has a good sound and communicates a clear, forceful picture. Record an agreed-upon line; ask students to determine necessary punctuation as you go along. Then ask for a third line composed of -ing words, again trying out lines and thinking about punctuation while recording. Ask students to think of a last line by brainstorming what the horse is, stands for, or is like. Again, the group should decide which line of those given is to be recorded.

4. Guide students in editing their final production--adding phrases and changing words to produce a more striking effect. Results produced by one college group are as follows:

Horse:

Sleek, fast, free,

Running, racing, prancing in the wild--

A thinker, alone.

5. Have one student lead the class in doing the nature thought as a choral speaking to the accompaniment of the recording used as background music during the story listening.

6. Ask students to form three- or four-person work teams to identify language learnings being developed through an integrated language experience of the type they just experienced. Have each work team print the learnings on large charting paper and post the chart somewhere in the room. Suggest that everyone study all the charts to see if there is some way to group the learnings into related clusters or categories. Have work teams reassemble to complete this task and report back on the clusters of language learnings they have discovered. Later the entire class can generalize about the nature of language learnings in elementary schools and how those learnings can be acquired. Guide students to consider the integration of language learnings possible through this approach, the importance of oral language in the experience, and the role of literature in the experience.

D. Experiencing Language Activity as Part of Content-Area Learning

In the same way, pre- and in-service teachers need some direct involvement in language learning as part of content-area study. Here is a lesson sequence to use with teachers to achieve this end.

1. Demonstrate to pre- or in-service teachers a common phenomenon, such as the attraction of certain materials to magnets, just as a fifth-grade teacher might do. As part of the demonstration, encourage participants to describe orally what is happening and also to develop a chartlike grid of materials that are attracted and are not attracted to a magnet. Use a variety of materials and magnets of different sizes and shapes. Most college science education departments have a collection of such magnets.

2. Demonstrate the lines of force around a magnet by shaking iron filings on a piece of paper laid on top of a horseshoe magnet. Do the same with two bar magnets; first set north pole to south pole, and then set north pole to north pole. Again stress talking about what is happening in each instance. Inject such words as <u>north pole</u>, <u>south pole</u>, <u>attract</u>, <u>repel</u>, and <u>lines of force</u>. As these words are used, record them on the board, especially noting the two syllables in the words <u>attract</u> and <u>repel</u> and the double consonants in the middle of <u>attract</u>. Have participants record these words in a notebook glossary complete with definitions.

3. Read aloud a brief selection on magnets from a trade or elementary science book. Suggest that participants listen to find out more facts about magnets that they have not already talked about as part of the demonstrations. Ask participants to jot at least one such point in their notebooks as they listen.

4. Follow the listening time with "factstorming," in which participants call out their points and scribes record them on the board. Later ask participants to group all points recorded on the board, including those recorded earlier, into related categories. To get the categorizing started, ask: Is there another point on the board that is on the same subtopic about magnets as this one? In this way, organize the points into clusters.

5. Next, involve participants in teacher-guided group writing. Have them decide on that category of facts about magnets which would be the most logical one to use to build into a first paragraph to tell people about magnets. Have participants dictate sentences to go into the paragraph and record these statements on the board, as suggested. Go back with participants to edit and revise suggested sentences, just as Ms. Topping did in Chapter 1 of the text.

6. Follow up with three-person team writing of other paragraphs on magnets. Later have teams orally share their paragraphs. As teams read their paragraphs aloud, ask listeners to decide on the best order to organize paragraphs into a short report on magnets.

7. Proceed to debriefing. In groups, participants decide what specific language skills were being developed through the demonstration lesson sequence. Then have them outline steps in the lesson to come up with a model structure for teaching language skills in content areas. To do the latter task, participants may refer to the flow chart given in the first chapter of Communication in Action, fourth edition.

E. Laying Out Teaching Plans on Flow Charts

Working in teams, pre- and in-service teachers can outline in flow-chart style the Rosie's Walk vignette that opens the text chapter. A model for flow-chart development is given below. Propose that in each block of the flow chart, planners plot an activity and the learnings emanating from it. The structure for the flow chart will look something like this:

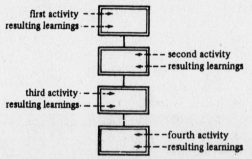

Use the resulting planning flow charts to have participants do the following:

1. Generalize about the nature of planning for language arts instruction.

2. Classify and generalize about the language learnings that emanate from a languaging-together time.

3. Generalize about the use of oral-language experiences in a language arts program.

4. Identify specific language teaching strategies.

If time permits, participants in the languaging-together time described under C and D above can outline schematically the plan for the session.

F. Analysis of Literature-Language Experience Approach

1. The <u>Rosie's Walk</u> and the melting/freezing episodes found in the first chapter of the text can serve as the basis for an analytical period during which students identify specific teaching strategies that are particularly applicable in language arts instruction. Strategies noted by the class can be recorded higgledy-piggledy on the chalkboard. Working from this firsthand data, two-person teams can:
   a. Identify the classroom areas and stations necessary for functional implementation of the approach.
   b. Design a classroom-space layout, or map, that provides functional working areas for carrying out these activities.

Provide large white construction paper for designs that can be posted around the room. Allow opportunity for "walking around and talking" so that students can cluster informally before the designs and make comparisons. Randomly select five students from different teams to explain and justify their layouts.

2. Or analyze the opening Teaching-in-Action episode with a class by asking questions like the following, in reference to Chapter 1, Masters 3 and 4. As students respond, record points directly on the Master projected as a transparency; students should record the points on individual copies you supply as a handout.
   a. What did Ms. Topping do to get her lesson off the ground? Why do you think she began in this way?
   b. What do you think was the purpose of having children first retell story events in order? of having children draw pictures of story events? of having them add relational words to their storymaps? of having individual children tell what was happening at key story points?
   c. Most teachers share pictures that accompany a storybook as they read the story. What was Ms. Topping trying to achieve by reserving picture interpretation until late in the experience?
   d. How did Ms. Topping blend written activity with oral activity?
   e. What kinds of writing activities did she include and in what sequence?
   f. What was the sequence of events that Ms. Topping scheduled as part of her science lesson? What language skills did she stress as part of that lesson? Why do you think she did this?
   g. In what ways was the sequence with <u>Rosie's Walk</u> similar to the sequence on melting and freezing? In what ways were the sequences different?
   h. How did Ms. Topping use textbooks in teaching? computers? other books and materials?
   i. Would you enjoy teaching the way Ms. Topping does? Why or why not? What difficulties do you see in this approach? what advantages?

G. Questions That Relate to the Forum

After students have read the chapter, direct their attention to the Chapter Forum. As part of a teacher-guided discussion, ask:

1. What are Jerome Harste, Don Holdaway, and Ken Goodman saying about language arts instruction?

2. In what ways does Ms. Topping's teaching reflect Holdaway's and Goodman's beliefs about instruction of language arts?

3. What practical suggestions given in the chapter concur with Harste's, Holdaway's, and Goodman's theory of instruction? Describe these suggestions. Is there a point where the ideas given in the chapter differ from that theory?

4. What do you mean by <u>theory</u>? How is theory helpful to the classroom teacher?

H. Discussion of Lesson Planning

After students have read the chapter and perhaps experienced the first chapter of <u>Sarah Plain and Tall</u> as a read-aloud DLTA (as described in the introduction to this guide, involve them in a discussion of lesson planning, using the model lesson plan in Chapter 1, Master 5. Use the questions given here to guide the discussion, and write summary points directly on the projected transparency. Or make multiple copies of the transparency master and the questions. Ask students to answer the questions through small-group interaction, and write their answers on the lesson-plan guide at the point where they apply.

 1. What is the purpose of the statement of objectives at the beginning of the plan?

 2. What is this teacher trying to achieve with his or her anticipatory set?

 3. What advantages do you see in using the webbing device before listening and/or reading?

 4. Why do you think this teacher asked students to predict before listening?

 5. In what way is what the teacher did under "Instruction and Modeling" a "model"?

 6. What was this teacher trying to achieve with his or her data chart?

 7. How is what this teacher did related to his or her objectives?

 8. What is meant by <u>visualizing</u>?

 9. What is the purpose of guided practice in a lesson?

10. What was the teacher trying to achieve through the second data chart?

11. What advantages do you see in use of a data chart as in this lesson?

12. What is this teacher trying to achieve through his or her closing set?

13. What advantages do you see in the two follow-up activities? What do you believe the teacher is trying to achieve through them?

14. Why is it important to evaluate children's learning on a continuous basis as in this instance?

Note: Use Chapter 1, Masters 6 and 7 when you do Sarah, Plain and Tall as a read-aloud.

I. Writing Lesson Plans

Suggest that students select a book to use with children as part of a read-aloud structured as a DLTA with predictions and verification of predictions as in the sample lesson plan. As an individual assignment or a group activity, have students plot out a lesson plan based on the book. Possible books include Log Cabin in the Woods by Joanne Henry and illustrated by Joyce Zarins (Macmillan, 1988), Owl Moon by Jane Yolen and illustrated by John Schoenherr (Philomel, 1987), Susanna of the Alamo by John Jakes (Gulliver/HBJ, 1986), and The Village of Round and Square Houses by Ann Grifalconi (Little, Brown, 1986) or a chapter from Charlotte's Web by E.B. White (Harper & Row, 1952) or Little House on the Prairie by Laura Ingalls Wilder (Harper & Row, 1935).

J. Reporting on Individual and Group Activities

Class members can present individual reports or brief panel discussions on related readings, such as the following:

Altwerger, Bess, Carole Edelsky, and Barbara Flores. "Whole Language: What's New?" The Reading Teacher, 41(November 1987): 144-154.

Cairney, Trevor, and Susan Langbien. "Building Communities of Readers and Writers." The Reading Teacher, 42(April 1989): 560-567.

Chatterton, Sharron. "On Becoming Teacher Experts: A Small Flight of Fancy on a Lesson." Language Arts, 64(September 1987): 540-542.

Clarke, Mark. "Don't Blame the System: Constraints on 'Whole Language' Reform." Language Arts, 64(April 1987): 384-396.

Clay, Marie. "Constructive Processes: Talking, Reading, Writing, Art, and Craft." The Reading Teacher, 39(April 1986): 764-770.

Clem, Chrisina, and Karen Feathers. "I LIC SPIDRS: What One Child Teaches Us about Content Learning." Language Arts, 63(February 1986): 143-147.

Cordeiro, Patricia. "Moonwatching: Learning and Teaching as a Scientific Enterprise." Language Arts, 63(February 1986): 148-152.

Crowell, Doris, et al. "Emerging Literacy: Reading-Writing Experiences in a Kindergarten Classroom." The Reading Teacher, 40(November 1986): 144-149.

Greene, Maxine. "Research Currents: What Are the Language Arts For?" Language Arts, 65(September 1988): 474-481.

Gunderson, Lee. "Whole Language Instruction: Writing in the 1st Grade." The Reading Teacher, 41 (January 1988): 430-437.

Lamme, Linda. "Authorship: A Key Facet of Whole Language." The Reading Teacher, 42(May 1989): 704-710.

Shanahan, Timothy. "The Reading-Writing Relationships: Seven Instructional Principles." The Reading Teacher, 41 (March 1988): 636-647.

Strickland, Dorothy, and Bernice Cullinan. "Literature and Language." Language Arts, 61(March 1986): 221-225.

Weiss, Jerry. "Writers and Readers: The Literary Connection." The Reading Teacher, 39(April 1986): 758-763.

Wicklund, LaDonna. "Shared Poetry: A Whole Language Experience for Remedial Readers." The Reading Teacher, 42(March 1989): 478-481.

IV. EXAMINATION QUESTIONS

A. Short Discussion Questions

1. Give four fundamental beliefs about language arts instruction as set forth in Communication in Action. For each, explain how you think that belief will affect your teaching. Then propose a fifth belief that you have arrived at yourself based on your study and thinking. Explain why you think that belief is significant.

2. Describe how you could teach language arts even as you are teaching a social studies lesson at the fifth-grade level. Include in your discussion the objectives you hope to achieve.

3. Explain the function of each of these elements of a lesson plan:
   a. Objectives
   b. Anticipatory Set
   c. Modeling
   d. Guided Practice
   e. Closing Set
   f. Follow-up Activities
   g. Evaluation

4. Open your text to the lesson plan for Sarah, Plain and Tall. Using it as a model, write a plan for sharing a storybook you like.

5. Describe how you would use each of these in language arts teaching:
   a. Trade books, such as Sarah, Plain and Tall.
   b. Basal reading books
   c. Subject-matter textbooks
   d. Computers

6. You are teaching a unit on the oceans to fourth-graders. Describe three language arts-oriented activities you could use as part of this unit. Be specific.

B. Multiple-Choice Questions

1. The whole-language approach stresses that
   a. Children acquire language facility by practicing discrete subskills.
   b. Children learn to use language as separate skill areas marked <u>reading, listening, speaking, writing</u>, and <u>thinking</u>.
   c. Children learn to use language through natural social interaction in which they create and communicate meanings.
   d. Children learn to use language through lessons in formal grammar through which they develop an understanding of their language.

2. Whole-language theorists believe that
   a. Children should be involved in language learning as part of their study of science but not of their study of mathematics.
   b. Children should be involved in language learning as part of their study of history but not of their study of music.
   c. Children should be involved in language learning as part of their study of history but not of their study of science.
   d. Communication should be the integrating thread in the elementary curriculum.

3. Which of the following represents a fundamental belief undergirding language arts instruction, as described in your text?
   a. Classroom activity is best pursued on a one-to-one basis.
   b. Classroom activity is best carried out in small groups--both teacher-guided and independent groups.
   c. Classroom activity is best pursued in large, class-size groups.
   d. Classroom activity should provide opportunities for social interaction in all its forms.

4. How do most language arts specialists view oral-language activity?
   a. As the connecting thread between reading and writing.
   b. As a less important dimension of elementary language arts than reading and writing.
   c. As a skill to be studied after learning to read and write.
   d. As a skill to be learned after learning to read.

5. What is the relationship between reading facility and oral-language activity?
   a. Oral-language activity bears no relationship to reading facility, since reading is based on the written language.
   b. Oral-language activity bears only a limited relationship to reading facility.
   c. Oral-language activity relates directly to reading facility.
   d. Oral-language activity and reading activity are completely opposite processes.

6. According to Vygotsky, what is the greatest discovery of a child's life?
   a. Each thing has its own name.
   b. Books hold hidden delight.
   c. Language play is fun.
   d. He or she is part of the human race.

7. Most theorists characterize thought primarily as
   a. A physical activity.
   b. A verbal activity.
   c. A visual activity.
   d. An emotional activity.

8. Educators today believe that children should
   a. Wait to write until they have learned how to read.
   b. Wait to read until they have learned to write.
   c. Wait to read and write until they have control over oral language.
   d. Be involved in reading and writing in a natural way from their earliest years.

9. Today, educators tend to view reading and writing as
   a. Opposite processes.
   b. Distinctive processes.
   c. Opposite and distinctive processes.
   d. Parts of one whole.

10. Which of the following is a good context for language learning in classrooms?
    a. As children make content-area investigations.
    b. As children read and listen to fine literature.
    c. As children engage in language play.
    d. As children experience life and people firsthand.
    e. All of the above.

11. The phrase language play means
    a. Playing orally with the sounds, meanings, and functions of words.
    b. Brainstorming words to find ones to use in communicating.
    c. Playing orally with sentences.
    d. All of the above.

12. What is a function of full-class instruction in a language arts program?
    a. It serves as the unifying experience of language-literature cycles.
    b. It meets individual language needs of students.
    c. It is the time for students to pursue personalized interests.
    d. It allows students to work at their own speeds.
    e. All of the above.

13. What is a learning center?
    a. A classroom where literature is the center of language learning.
    b. A classroom where oral language is paramount.
    c. A classroom area where several related tasks are assembled.
    d. The central area of classroom space from which the teacher guides children's learning.
    e. The central area of classroom space cleared for dramatic activity.

14. A statement of specific learnings to be achieved through instruction is called
    a. An anticipatory set.
    b. A closing set.
    c. An objective.
    d. A guided practice activity.
    e. A follow-up activity.

15. What is the function of an anticipatory set?
    a. It sets students' minds to the one way to view a topic.
    b. It focuses attention on what is to be learned.
    c. It states the specific learning to be achieved.
    d. It models what students will do or how they will think through a problem.

16. Of the following, which is the most accurate generalization about successful lessons?
    a. Each lesson should be considered a discrete entity.
    b. Lessons should be based on meaningful content.
    c. All lessons should be set up in learning stations to foster independent learning.
    d. Children should study individually without making oral contact with one another.
    e. All lessons should have a literature component.

17. What is the first step a teacher takes in planning an effective lesson?
    a. Identifying materials needed.
    b. Listing key strategies to employ.
    c. Identifying effective evaluative devices to use.
    d. Identifying learnings to be acquired.

18. Of the following, which is identified in your text as an _unproductive_ way of using language arts textbooks in elementary schools?
    a. As a source of word and sentence material.
    b. As an introduction to language and literature study.
    c. As the content for personalized learning by students needing additional practice.

19. Of the following, which cognitive process is central in a DLTA or DRTA?
    a. Predicting.
    b. Evaluating.
    c. Explaining.
    d. Describing.

20. Of the following, which does your text highlight as the most significant and creative application of the microcomputer to language arts programs?
    a. CAI.
    b. CMI.
    c. Word processing and desk-top publishing.
    d. Learning to program in a computer language.

CHAPTER 2

LANGUAGE AND CHILDREN'S LANGUAGE DEVELOPMENT--
WHERE COMMUNICATION IS IN ACTION

I.   CHAPTER THEMES--WHAT IS INTENDED

Chapter 2 explains how children build conceptual meaning, develop the ability
to communicate and think, and grow in cognitive ability. Additionally, it
describes four aspects of language children must master to communicate: words,
syntax, intonation patterns, and kinesic behavior. Finally, the chapter sets
forth another way of knowing a language--knowing the history of it--and
provides ideas for helping children understand the antecedents of their
language.

II.   CHAPTER GOALS--WHAT IS TO BE LEARNED

Having read the chapter and completed the skill-building activities, one should
be able to state:

    I can use the words <u>assimilation</u>, <u>accommodation</u>, and <u>schemata</u> in
explaining how children build meaningful concepts.

    I can distinguish among egocentric, socialized, and inner speech, and can
list ways to build socialized and inner speech in classrooms.

    I can outline the stages of cognitive development as set forth by Piaget.

    I can explain verbal and nonverbal patterns of language and how children
learn those patterns.

    I can define terms used to talk about language: <u>phoneme</u>, <u>grapheme</u>,
<u>morpheme</u>, <u>stress</u>, <u>juncture</u>, and <u>syntax</u>.

    I can outline major generalizations about the history of English and
describe ways of involving children with them.

III. IDEAS FOR CREATIVE ENCOUNTERS WITH LANGUAGE AND WITH INSTRUCTIONAL
      STRATEGIES

A. Survey of Chapter 2

Ask students to brainstorm ideas that come to mind relative to the chapter
title and to record those ideas above the title web on the first page of the
chapter. Encourage students to survey the chapter headings and the summary
paragraph at the end of the chapter and to write questions or predictions to
guide their reading. Have them write these items beneath the title web from
lines attached to it. Remind students that in college texts there is often
space around the title where they can record "Getting Ready to Read" notes.
Tell them that they can use a similar "Getting Ready to Read" strategy as
children prepare to read a selection from a content-area textbook except that
youngsters create their prereading webs on paper, not in their books. Use
Chapter 2, Master 1 to guide the prereading study when pursued as a class
activity, and record brainstormed ideas on it as students write their notes in
their books.

B. Analysis of Initial Teaching Episode

Pre- and in-service teachers should be aware that the language teaching
strategies they employ give evidence of the assumptions about language learning
they hold. To begin to relate teaching strategies and assumptions, students
should be asked to identify the assumptions underlying Ms. Morris's teaching as
described at the beginning of Chapter 2. Since even graduate students may need
guidance in identifying assumptions, you can structure this session by asking:

1. Why did Ms. Morris begin her Yellow Ball Afternoon with choral speaking and
talking-together? What did she want to achieve at this point?

2. What assumption did Ms. Morris have in mind when she next had the children
play with pair, pear, and pare? Why do you think she taught the differences
among the words in the way she did rather than have the youngsters fill in
workbook blanks?

3. Based on Ms. Morris's other classroom actions, what additional assumptions
can you identify?

4. What relationships exist between assumptions and actions?

Project Chapter 2, Master 2 as a transparency during the discussion. Have
volunteers add assumptions to the transparency.

C.   Reviewing Theories about Language Learning

Assign small segments of the chapter to individual students, who must be ready
to explain to a small task group the key points made in the assigned segment.
Segments to assign are "Concept Formation and Vocabulary Development,"
"Development of Communication and Thinking Power," "Children's Cognitive
Development," "Words," "Syntax," "Vocal Intonation," and "Nonverbal Language."
Divide the class into seven-person groups, with one member of each group taking
responsibility for one of the assignment segments and explaining it to his or

her fellow group members. Listeners and/or readers can use Chapter 2, Master 3, DATA RETRIEVAL CHART--LANGUAGE DEVELOPMENT, for recording main ideas and terms. Make a transparency from the master to project and complete during a follow-up, total-class summary discussion. Use Chapter 2, Master 4 during the discussion.

D. Questions That Relate to the Chapter Forums

These questions can be used as the basis for a teacher-guided class discussion or an independent small-group discussion followed by reporting.

1. What is meant by an interactive view of language development as discussed by Lindfors and Bissex?

2. From your reading of the chapter, explain how social interaction relates to children's acquisition of concepts and vocabulary, syntax, intonation, and nonverbal behaviors.

3. What do Corson and Moffett have to say about inner speech? How does inner speech relate to thought? to reading? to writing? When have you used (or do you use) inner speech in thinking? in reading? in writing?

E. Identifying and Rank-Ordering Learnings

As a class, brainstorm the specific learnings subsumed under "knowing a language" and under "knowing about language." Two class scribes can record brainstormed items under appropriate labels on the chalkboard. Then students, in five-person teams, rank-order the specific items from most to least significant. Suggest to students that items may be ranked equally. Next, groups share their final rankings and present their supporting arguments. The seminar session can be completed by generalizing about the relative importance of "knowing how" and "knowing about" as they relate to language learning.

F. Analyzing Language Arts Programs in Terms of "Knowing How" and "Knowing About"

Some publishers of language arts text series will supply scope and sequence charts in classroom quantity for use by pre- and in-service teachers. Working in teams, class members can analyze, compare, and contrast charts from several text series in terms of the emphasis given to "knowing how" and "knowing about."

G. Reporting on Individual and Group Activities

Individual reports and panel discussions can develop from the following independent readings:

Dyson, Anne, and Celia Dyson. "Research Currents: Children's Language for Learning," Language Arts, 60(September 1983): 751-757.

Early Childhood and Literacy Development Committee of the International Reading
     Association. "IRA Position Statement on Reading and Writing in Early
     Childhood." The Reading Teacher, 39(April 1986): 822-824.

Early Childhood and Literacy Development Committee of the International Reading
     Association. "Joint Statement on Literacy Development and Pre-first
     Grade." The Reading Teacher, 39(April 1986): 819-821.

Fox, Sharon. "Research Update: Oral Language Development." Language Arts,
     60(February 1983): 234-243.

Genishi, Celia. "Research Currents: What Is a Context for Learning through
Language?" Language Arts, 61(January 1984): 52-58.

Moffett, James. "Reading and Writing as Meditation." Language Arts, 60(March
     1983): 315-322.

Strickland, Dorothy, and Lesley Morrow. "Young Children's Early Writing
     Development." The Reading Teacher, 42(February 1989): 426-427.

Walters, Keith, et al. "Formal and Functional Approaches to Literacy."
     Language Arts, 64(December 1987): 855-868.

IV. EXAMINATION QUESTIONS

A. Short Discussion Questions

1.   Explain what is meant by a Yellow Ball Afternoon. Then explain the major
      purpose of such an experience in the elementary language arts program.

2.   Describe the manner in which young children build functional concepts.
      In your description use the terms accommodation, assimilation, and
      schemata.

3.   Draw a diagram that shows the relationship among egocentric, socialized,
      and interiorized speech. Add a brief caption that sums up the
      relationship.

4.   Briefly describe two activities through which children can build
      socialized speech in classrooms.

5.   Distinguish among phoneme, grapheme, and morpheme.

6.   The text describes four aspects of language that are important in
      communication. Rank-order the four according to their importance in
      communicating. Then present a short rationale supporting your proposed
      order. You may assign an identical ranking to one or more of the aspects
      if you see fit.

7.   Give one major generalization about the nature of language. Then
      describe one way through which you could help students build their
      understanding of this generalization.

B. Multiple-Choice Questions

1. In the pair of sentences "I saw John" and "John saw me," a difference in meaning is communicated primarily through a difference in
    a. Phonemes.
    b. Morphemes.
    c. Syntax.
    d. Stress.
    e. Juncture.

2. In the pair of words <u>pen</u> and <u>men</u>, a difference in meaning is communicated primarily through a difference in
    a. Phonemes.
    b. Morphemes.
    c. Syntax.
    d. Stress.
    e. Juncture.

3. Language development theorists believe that language learning is a matter of
    a. Acquiring the ability to use and interpret the deep structure of language.
    b. Memorizing the rules for sentence making.
    c. Memorizing heard sentences to be used on later occasions.
    d. Memorizing definitions of words.

4. A child points to a melon and says, "Ball." Mother answers, "That's a melon, not a ball." At this point, the child is building a concept of ball through the process of
    a. Interiorized speech.
    b. Accommodation.
    c. Association.
    d. Questioning.

5. <u>Repetition</u>, <u>monologue</u>, and <u>collective monologue</u> are terms applied to
    a. Inner speech.
    b. Interiorized speech.
    c. Socialized speech.
    d. Egocentric speech.

6. The ability to use words is important in
    a. Thinking.
    b. Communicating.
    c. Thinking and communicating.

7. Your text proposes that teachers encourage children to
    a. Talk out loud as part of problem solving.
    b. Talk to the self whisper-style when a job gets tough.
    c. Tell themselves stories read or heard.
    d. All of the above.

8. <u>Communication</u> is derived from the Latin word <u>communicare</u>, meaning to
   a. Share or make common.
   b. Receive.
   c. Meditate.
   d. Carry away.
   e. Know.

9. In the classic study of the child and chimp reared together, the chimp
   kept up with the child until the child began to
   a. Walk.
   b. Use words.
   c. Crawl.
   d. Recognize his or her mother.
   e. Smile.

10. All languages share certain syntactic features. They
    a. Have rules for converting statements into questions.
    b. Rely on noun and verb phrases as the basis for sentence construction.
    c. Have words used to modify nouns and verbs.
    d. All of the above.
    e. None of the above.

11. Grammaticalness is judged in terms of
    a. Proper pronunciation of spoken words.
    b. Conformity to the sentence-making rules of language.
    c. Proper punctuation and spelling.
    d. Adherence to traditional usage patterns.
    e. c and d.
    f. All of the above.

12. Students in schools study the grammar of their language in order to
    a. Speak more effectively.
    b. Write more effectively.
    c. Read more efficiently.
    d. Communicate with greater effectiveness.
    e. Understand and appreciate the marvelous way language operates.

13. Stress, pitch, and juncture are features of
    a. Morphology.
    b. Syntax.
    c. Kinesic behavior.
    d. Vocal intonation.

14. For the writer to punctuate sentence endings accurately, he or she must
    a. Know the definition of a sentence.
    b. Be able to define the four kinds of sentences--declarative,
       imperative, exclamatory, and interrogative.
    c. Be able to distinguish the sounds of sentences and translate those
       sounds into punctuation marks.
    d. All of the above.

15. Of the following statements about kinesic behavior, which is *not* true?
    a. Body languages are as numerous as verbal languages.
    b. A kinesic behavior has a single and universal meaning.
    c. Kinesic behavior is often used as an adjunct to verbal language.
    d. Kinesic behaviors can communicate without any accompanying speech.
    e. Kinesic behaviors are used sometimes when a message is too sensitive for verbal expression.

16. What is an ideograph?
    a. An idea expressed in the form of a bar graph.
    b. An idea expressed in the form of a line graph.
    c. A highly stylized picture that represents a thought.
    d. A clear and representational picture that stands for a thought.
    e. A pictograph.

17. Of the following statements about language, which one is *least* correct?
    a. Acceptable usage may become unacceptable.
    b. Unacceptable usage may become acceptable.
    c. Dictionaries as records of spelling, meaning, and pronunciation are unchanging.
    d. New words are constantly being added to languages to meet new demands.
    e. Some words drop from common usage as the need for them lessens.

18. The <u>least</u> desirable form that language study can take is
    a. Involving children in language comparison studies.
    b. Involving children in word searches.
    c. Integrating language study with social science study.
    d. Sharing interesting material by telling and explaining it to children.

19. Piaget refers to the period when a child begins to handle language in an abstract way as the
    a. Formal operational stage.
    b. Preoperational stage.
    c. Concrete operational stage.
    d. Sensorimotor stage.

20. Social interaction is important in children's development of
    a. Oral-language facility.
    b. Reading facility.
    c. Writing facility.
    d. All of the above.

CHAPTER 3

LITERATURE IN THE LANGUAGE ARTS--
WHERE CHILDHOOD'S DREAMS ARE TWINED

I. CHAPTER THEMES--WHAT IS INTENDED

Chapter 3 provides a brief survey of children's literature so that teachers
will have a knowledge base for making choices about books to use as
springboards into language experience and as suggestions for independent
reading.

II. CHAPTER GOALS--WHAT IS TO BE LEARNED

Having read the chapter and completed the skill-building activities at the end
of each section, one should be able to state the following:

     I can explain how character, plot, theme, verbal style, and pictorial
style work together in literature children enjoy.

     I can describe ways to release the positive potential of books, such as
word plays, adventures with sentence patterns, the modeling of stories after
those read, picture interpretation, dramatics, and the exploration of themes
and topics.

     I can recognize sexual, racial, and religious stereotypes found in some
books.

III. IDEAS FOR CREATIVE ENCOUNTERS WITH LANGUAGE AND WITH INSTRUCTIONAL
       STRATEGIES

A. Survey of Chapter 3

Ask students to brainstorm ideas that come to mind relative to the chapter
title and to record those ideas above the title web on the first page of the
chapter. Encourage students to survey the chapter headings and the summary
paragraph at the end of the chapter and to write questions or predictions to
guide their reading. Have them write these items beneath the title web from
lines attached to it. Remind students that in college texts there is often
space around the title where they can record "Getting Ready to Read" notes.
Tell them that they can use a similar "Getting Ready to Read" strategy as
children prepare to read a selection from a content-area textbook, except that
youngsters create their prereading webs on paper, not in their books. Use

Chapter 3, Master 1 to guide the prereading study when pursued as a class activity, and record brainstormed ideas on it as students write their notes in their books.

B. Analyzing Books Together--A Series of Sessions

1. Read aloud a classic picture storybook, such as <u>Madeline's Rescue</u> by Ludwig Bemelmans (Viking, 1951) or <u>Jumanji</u> by Chris Van Allsburg (Houghton Mifflin, 1981). Ask students to look and listen for elements of language use, plot, theme, character, and illustration that produce an effective impact. Be sure to display the pictures as you go along, and use your body and voice to convey mood and action, for especially with undergraduate education majors, the instructor's manner of story sharing serves as a model. Have students follow this listening-together time with a sharing-of-thoughts time in which they identify and share specific elements noted.

2. Share the pictures and story from several books, such as Sendak's <u>Where the Wild Things Are</u> (Harper & Row, 1963), De Regnier's <u>May I Bring a Friend</u>? (Atheneum, 1974), Van Allsburg's <u>The Polar Express</u> (Houghton Mifflin, 1985), Younk's <u>Hey, Al</u> (Farrar, Straus and Giroux, 1986), and Ackerman's <u>Song and Dance Man</u> (Knopf, 1988). One way to share is through the short iconographic films produced by Weston Woods and Miller-Brody. Listener-viewers compare and contrast the varying styles of the pictures and consider ways in which the pictures in each selection harmonize with the story.

3. Show first a sound filmstrip, and then the sound film, for a picture storybook. Particularly good for this purpose are filmstrips/films from Weston Woods. Follow the back-to-back viewing by having students, in small groups, engage in a short analysis in which they consider the following:
    a. What is the strength of the filmed version? the weakness?
    b. What is the strength of the filmstrip version? the weakness?
    c. What would be a particularly good use of the filmed version?
    d. What would be a particularly good use of the filmstrip version?
    e. How can you relate the film or filmstrip to the book itself?
These questions can be duplicated as a Task Sheet to be distributed prior to group activity.

4. A seminar session can be structured around controversial children's books. Have pre- or in-service teachers prepare for the session by reading at least one book. During the session, have participants contribute brief statements about the content of the books they read and cooperatively formulate conclusions about how and when and to use those books. A similar session can be based on the children's books described in Chapter 3 of the text, with each participant reading one book and orally describing such key aspects as theme, verbal and pictorial styles, plot, and characterization.

5. Share selected paragraphs from a book having strong characterization. Read aloud a paragraph or two; have students listen to identify adjectives to describe a main character and then give their adjectives, which you can record on the chalkboard. Read another paragraph or two; again have students listen to identify other adjectives to describe the character. After students have listened to five or six segments in this manner, ask them to generalize about what good story characters are all about--for example, multidimensional, human yet larger than life, consistent and predictable to some extent, emotionally grabbing. Stories that this author has used successfully in this way are

Mildred Taylor's <u>Role of Thunder, Hear My Cry</u> (Dial, 1976) and <u>The Friendship</u> (Dial, 1988) and Pamela Travers's <u>Mary Poppins</u> (Bucaneer Books, 1981). This activity not only teaches students about characterization in children's books but also models a way to handle characterization with upper-graders.

6. Share selected paragraphs from a book such as E.L. Konigsburg's <u>Jennifer, Hecate, Macbeth, William McKinley & Me, Elizabeth</u> (Atheneum, 1967) that has clear descriptions of a character (in this case, Jennifer), striking dialogue, and good plot development. Have students in college classes listen to identify those elements of the author's verbal style which make it so distinctive-- humor,clarity of description, excitement, short-long sentence contrasts, and so forth. This activity helps students understand some elements of verbal style and models for them ways to involve children in these elements. Use Sid Fleischman's <u>The Whipping Boy</u> (Greenwillow, 1986) in a similar way.

7. Orally share segments of a story, following the directions in Chapter 3, Master 2. Stopping periodically, ask volunteers to provide a description of the event they have just heard, their analysis of the character's feelings, and their own feelings. Record these comments on the projected transparency. Use intermediate-level books for this purpose. Use Chapter 3, Master 3 in a similar way, this time asking students to listen to make predictions about what will happen in the story.

8. Use Chapter 3, Master 4 to summarize elements important in a story. First, read aloud a storybook such as Mordicai Gerstein's <u>The Mountains of Tibet</u> (Harper & Row, 1988). Then have students work in groups to identify the setting, characters, plot, theme, and verbal style of the story and reflect on the significance of each of these elements in that story. Schedule a follow-up class discussion.

9. Use Chapter 3, Master 5 as the basis for an assignment. Ask students to locate a story that falls into each category. Schedule a small-group sharing period in which students report on the stories they have found.

C. Using Books as a Stepping Stone into Language and Creative Expression

Involve pr- and in-service teachers directly in a language-learning experience with a book serving as a steppingstone into creative expression. The sequence detailed below can be used in association with Chapters 4 and/or 5 as a lead into consideration of listening and speaking.

1. Read aloud Eric Carle's <u>The Rooster Who Set Out to See the World</u> (Franklin Watts, 1972), showing the pictures as you read along. Follow story listening by building with listeners a story staircase. Start by sketching an empty staircase on the chalkboard or on charting paper. Then have volunteers add sketches to show each step in the story sequence. Follow with an oral sharing of <u>Henny Penny</u>; ask participants to listen to find out how <u>Henny</u> is similar to the first story heard and how it is different. Guide participants to identify such similarities and differences as the following:
   a. Both start as come-along stories with more and more characters joining an original one.
   b. Both have animal characters who speak.
   c. The specific characters in each are different.
   d. The reason animals come along is different in each story.

Now ask participants to form three-person teams, each to constructing a story staircase for <u>Henny Penny</u> and to share the construction with the class.

2. Return to the collages in <u>The Rooster</u>. Give participants time to examine the collages closely, especially the one of the rooster that shows rather clearly the method through which it was produced. Suggest to participants that they can produce animal pictures through the same method--collage. Using large white construction paper, quickly sketch a rooster shape modeled after the one in the Carle book. Dab colored tempera with a brush onto blue tissue paper. Then cut out a tail-feather shape from the paint-dabbed paper and stick it onto the tail section of your rooster sketch. Ask participants to consider how other animals in the book were created, to clarify the steps in the production of a collage: (a) sketch a proposed animal on large white construction paper, (b) choose basic colors to add to the animal and dab tempera on appropriately colored tissue paper, and (c) cut out shapes from the dabbed tissue paper and paste them on the original animal shape.

    Once participants have analyzed the picture style and production method, have them form five-person task forces, each given the task of deciding on an interesting animal to create and cooperatively producing it. Upon completion of the project, teams should cut their animal creatures out of the white background and mount them on a classroom bulletin board on which you have stapled a light background.

3. During a follow-up session, review the characteristics of a come-along story, perhaps by sharing another one that adheres to the same motif, such as Mirra Ginsburg's <u>How the Sun Was Brought Back to the Sky</u> (Macmillan, 1975). Propose that the class cooperate in the oral creation of an original come-along story using the animals already mounted on the bulletin board as story characters. As a group, decide which animal will function as the main character and what that character will ask the others to come along and do. You may wish to string a piece of colored yarn from left to right across the board and mount the main character piece on the left end of the yarn. Guide participants to think about the order in which the other character pieces will enter the story, and mount the pieces in the predetermined order from left to right along the yarn. (You might ask college-level participants to think about a come-along initiation that the main character could repeat to each character encountered in turn). Ask participants to brainstorm possible story endings and select one. Then have them create the specific lines for their original story, with individual volunteers orally contributing lines.

4. For follow-up, if time permits, have college-level students, working in teams, (a) write down the class story, (b) create story staircases for other come-along stories they will originate and share orally with the class group, (c) write out original come-along stories, and (d) make tape recordings of the class's come-along story.

5. Allow considerable time for a class or small-group discussion of the language-literature experience in which teachers have participated directly. Ask participants to identify the following:
   a. The assumptions about learning, instruction, language, and literature underlying the use of such an experience with elementary students.
   b. The language learnings developed through the experience.
   c. Other learnings that will result.

d. The planning scheme for the experience, shown flow-chart-style as developed in Chapter 1 of this guide.

e. The grade level at which such an experience might be applicable.

f. Ways in which the experience might be simplified for use at lower levels. (One way is to have children draw and color an animal with a flow-pen or a crayon--something you may have to resort to with teachers if tempera, brushes, and time are limited or unavailable.)

To facilitate the discussion, you can convert items a-f above into a group discussion guide to duplicate and distribute. To make this discussion work, however, participants should have had prior experience in identifying assumptions and outlining planning schemes as set forth in Chapters 1 and 2 of this guide.

D. Learning in Learning Stations

Because there are so many literature-related materials available today, you may wish to set up some learning stations to which students have access during out-of-class hours or to which students go on a rotation basis during class hours. Given the availability of materials, you can set up the following:

1. Several sound-filmstrip stations at which students, in three- or four-person teams, view sound strips of picture storybooks available from Miller-Brody, Western Woods, and other companies. Each station should contain a tape recorder, a filmstrip viewer, headphones, the tape and filmstrip package, and the accompanying book. The Task Sheet entitled "Analyzing Sound Filmstrips That Accompany Picture Storybooks," found in the Appendices, can serve as directions.

2. Several story-tape or -record stations at which participants listen to professionally told stories, such as those available through Caedmon.

3. Several storybook stations at which participants scan and talk about collections of children's books gathered there.

E. Questions That Relate to the Chapter Forum

These questions may be used as the basis for a teacher-guided class discussion or a small-group interaction after students have read the chapter.

1. What does Louis Rosenblatt mean by the term poem? How is the poem different from the text? What does a reader do when he or she reads a text? What does this theory of literary transaction imply about classroom literary experiences? What kinds of literary experiences could and should you as a teacher provide for your students? Think about this last question by considering specific activities and ideas offered in Chapter 3.

2. According to Lee Galda, how can a teacher limit students' responses to literature? extend it? How did the teacher in the opening vignette extend Amy's response?

F. Reporting on Individual and Group Activities

Class members can present individual reports or panel discussions based on the following readings:

Bauman, Marcy. "Literature, Repetition, and Meaning." Language Arts, 64(January 1987): 54-60.

Brozo, William and Carl Tomlinson. "Literature: The Key to Lively Content Courses." The Reading Teacher, 40(December 1986): 288-293.

Butler, Dorothy. "Reading Begins at Home," Part I and II. The Horn Book, 59(October 1983): 545-552 and (December 1983):742-746.

Dougherty, Wilma, and Rosalind Engel. "An 80s Look for Sex Equality in Caldecott Winners and Honor Books." The Reading Teacher, 40(January 1987): 394-399.

Goldstone, Bette. "Visual Interpretation of Children's Books." The Reading Teacher, 42(April 1989): 592-595.

Hickman, Janet. "Research Currents: Researching Children's Response to Literature." Language Arts, 61(March 1984): 278-284.

Hill, Bonnie. "Books Before Five Revisited." Language Arts, 66(March 1989): 309-317.

L'Engle, Madeline. "Do I Disturb the Universe?" The Horn Book, 59(December 1983): 673-682.

Martinez, Miriam, and Nancy Roser. "Read It Again: The Value of Repeated Readings during Storytime." The Reading Teacher, 38(April 1985): 782-787.

Mikkelsen, Nina. "Talking and Telling: The Child as Storymaker." Language Arts, 61(March 1984): 229-239.

Piccolo, Jo Anne. "Writing a No-Fault Narrative: Every Teacher's Dream." The Reading Teacher, 40(November 1986): 136-142.

Reed, Arthea. Comics to Classics. Newark, Del.: International Reading Association, 1988.

Roser, Nancy. "Research Currents: Relinking Literature and Literacy." Language Arts, 64(January 1987): 90-97.

Roser, Nancy, and Georgene Wilson. "Books for Reading about Reading: Read-Alouds for Children Learning to Read." The Reading Teacher, 40(December 1986): 282-287.

Smith, Nancy, M. Jean Grenlaw, and Carolyn Scott. "Making the Literate Environmental Equitable." The Reading Teacher, 40(January 1987): 400-407.

Sullivan, Joanna. "Read Aloud Sessions: Tackling Sensitive Issues through Literature." The Reading Teacher, 40(May 1987): 874-878.

Tomlinson, Carl. "World Literature for and about Today's Children." The Reading Teacher, 40(October 1986): 120-121.

Van Dongen, Richard. "Children's Narrative Thought, at Home and at School." Language Arts 64(January 1987):79-87.

Wagner, Cindy. "Student-made Gameboards: A Response to Literature." The Reading Teacher, 40(February 1987): 581-582.

Wilson, Patricia. "What Children's Literature Classics Do Children Really Enjoy?" The Reading Teacher, 41(January 1988): 406-411.

G. Film Viewing

Films that relate to the content of Chapter 3 include:

Attic in the Wind. Weston Woods, Weston, Conn. Running time is 12 minutes.

The Lively Art of Picture Books. Weston Woods, Weston, Conn. Running time is 57 minutes.

Mr. Sheperd and Mr. Milne. Weston Woods, Weston, Conn. Running time is 29 minutes.

Paddle to the Sea. National Film Board of Canada. Running time is 28 minutes.

The Tale of the Lazy People. Miller-Brody. Running time is 20 minutes.

IV. EXAMINATION QUESTIONS

A. Short Discussion Questions

1. Explain how to use a book as a "natural vehicle for creative expression" by describing a specific example of a learning sequence you could develop that would spring out of an encounter with a book. Gear your sequence for upper-elementary students.

2. Describe briefly the qualities that make for a memorable story character. Indicate the one quality you feel is most essential and explain the reasons for your choice.

3. Explain what is meant by the term believability when applied to children's books. Use an example to clarify your explanation.

4. Write a paragraph in which you describe briefly the ways that master writers manipulate words and sounds to achieve striking effects.

5. Define the phrase episodic book, and explain the point at which this kind of book is particularly appealing to readers.

6. Name a book that you believe is particularly good for helping children grow in their appreciation of words. Then describe an activity through which you could use that book to involve children in word relationships.

7. Name a book that you believe is good to teach story design. Then describe
    how you would use that book to teach story design.

B. Multiple-Choice Questions

1. In books for younger children, one generally finds
    a. Characters who are more clearly delineated than those in books for
        older readers.
    b. Pictures playing a more significant role than they do in books for
        older readers.
    c. Plots composed of a number of subplots.
    d. All of the above.

2. Symbolic meanings are important in all books, but they are a fundamental
    aspect of
    a. Episodic books.
    b. Picture storybooks.
    c. Mysteries.
    d. Allegories.
    e. Adventure stories.

3. According to Anderson and Goff, "the foremost determinant of literary
    effectiveness" is
    a. Plot.
    b. Characters.
    c. Theme.
    d. Pictures.
    e. Language.

4. The Newbery Medal is awarded annually to
    a. The author who has made the most distinguished contribution to
        literature.
    b. The author who has made the most distinguished contribution to
        American literature for children.
    c. The artist of the most distinguished American picture book for
        children.
    d. The artist of the most distinguished picture book in the world.
    e. Both the author and the artist of the most distinguished book for
        children.

5. Pictures and story line in a picture storybook should harmonize in
    a. Size.
    b. Color.
    c. Detail.
    d. All of the above.

6. Reacting to sexism in children's literature, Charlotte Huck proposes that we
    a. Change the traditional folktales and fairy tales to reflect a more liberated point of view.
    b. No longer introduce children to folktales and fairy tales that project sex-role stereotypes.
    c. Continue to introduce children to traditional tales but simultaneously introduce them to literature projecting a broader view.
    d. Ignore the problem since children are unaware of it.

7. With regard to books children have read in the past, it is correct to say that
    a. Boys and girls have been equally dominant figures in nonfiction.
    b. Girls have been the dominant figures in most fiction selections.
    c. Boys are depicted in more active pursuits than girls.
    d. Girls are generally depicted in leadership roles.
    e   All of the above.

8. According to Charlotte Huck, the first question young readers ask about a book is
    a. Does it tell a good story?
    b. Are the characters likable?
    c. Are the characters believable?
    d. Are the words readable?
    e. Does it teach a worthwhile lesson?

9. A reader's response to literature grows out of
    a. His or her prior experiences with life, literature, and language.
    b. The author's skill in telling the story.
    c. Both a and b.

10. Of the following kinds of stories, which has an ending with a twist that the reader does not anticipate?
    a. A step-by-step story.
    b. A turn about story.
    c. A circular story.
    d. A just-imagine story.

11. How do literature specialists define the term theme?
    a. The underlying meaning that unifies a story.
    b. The plot.
    c. The setting.
    d. The dialogue.
    e. The interaction.

12. Of the following, which does your book identify as the least successful way to help children enjoy and understand the design of a story?
    a. Joining in to the telling of a story by predicting what will happen next.
    b. Creating stories of similar design.
    c. Mapping the happiness and sadness flow of a story.
    d. Using hand motions to clarify the design.
    e. Filling in the blanks of a story grid with key elements of the story.

13. Your text recommends that story encounters should involve children in
    a. Predicting.
    b. Comparing and contrasting.
    c. Relating story happenings to their own lives.
    d. All of the above.

14. Educators recommend that teachers orally share
    a. Storybooks with primary children.
    b. Story and informational books with primary children.
    c. Story and informational books with primary and intermediate children.
    d. Informational books with primary and intermediate children and
       storybooks with primary children.

15. Believability, as applied to stories, means that the
    a. Story events are very realistic and thus believable.
    b. Characters are very human and act realistically.
    c. Setting is realistic rather than fantastic.
    d. Story is believable even though unrealistic things happen.
    e. All of the above.

CHAPTER 4

LISTENING FOR MEANING--
LEARNING TO LISTEN AND LISTENING TO LEARN

I. CHAPTER THEMES--WHAT IS INTENDED

Chapter 4 defines active, purpose-filled listening and suggests specific ways
through which informational, critical-analytical, critical-judgmental, and
appreciative listening skills can be developed as part of ongoing classroom
activity and as part of encounters with literature, language, and the content
areas.

II. CHAPTER GOALS--WHAT IS TO BE LEARNED

Having read the chapter and completed the skill-building activities at the end
of each section, one should be able to state the following:

    I can explain how active, purpose-filled listening can be achieved in
elementary classrooms.

    I can identify specific informational listening skills and can design
classroom activities through which children can build and refine these skills.

    I can distinguish between analytical and judgmental listening skills. I
can identify the specific critical listening skills to be acquired and can
design action- and purpose-filled activities for building and refining these
skills.

    I can identify specific appreciative listening skills and can design
activities for building and refining these skills.

    I can use a check list to assess children's needs for more attention to
listening skills.

III. IDEAS FOR CREATIVE ENCOUNTERS WITH LANGUAGE AND WITH INSTRUCTIONAL
      STRATEGIES

A. Survey of Chapter 4

Ask student to brainstorm ideas that come to mind relative to the chapter title
and to record those ideas above the title web on the first page of the chapter.
Encourage students to survey the chapter headings and the summary paragraph at
the end of the chapter and to write questions or predictions to guide their

reading. Have them write these items beneath the title web from lines attached to it. Remind students that in college texts there is often space around the title where they can record "Getting Ready to Read" notes. Tell them that they can use a similar "Getting Ready to Read" strategy as children prepare to read a selection from a content-area textbook, except that youngsters create their prereading webs on paper, not in their books. Use Chapter 4, Master 1 to guide the prereading study when pursued as a class activity, and record brainstormed ideas on it as students write their notes in their books.

B. Analyzing the Teaching-in-Action Vignette--"Getting at the Root of Conflict"

Analyze the vignette that opens the chapter; do so through a total class discussion using the questions in Chapter 4, Master 2 or through small-group interaction. In the latter case, make copies of the master to distribute as a discussion guide, and follow with a total-class sharing time in which you project the master as a transparency.

C. Use Chapter 4, Master 3 as the basis of an introductory lesson on the kinds of listening. Have students scan their books to volunteer information to add to the data chart as you project it as a transparency. Students can add points directly to the transparency with a washable marker.

D. Looking at Listening in Action

Teachers who have participated in the literature-language experience based on The Rooster Who Set Out to See the World detailed in Chapter 3 of this guide can analyze that sequence of experiences in classroom teams by using this Task Sheet:

1. Identify those components of the experience with The Rooster which involved participants in conversational listening. What listening skills were being developed during these conversational listening times?

2. Identify those components of the experience which involved participants in presentational listening. What listening skills were being developed during these presentational listening times?

3. Identify those components which required an active listening response.

4. Identify those components which involved participants in informational listening, critical listening, and appreciative listening.

Teams can report their findings back to the class, with some concluding time being allocated to consideration of such questions as:

1. How can specific listening skills be achieved through literary experiences?

2. What is achieved through classroom presentational and conversational listening sessions?

3. What is the relationship between teaching listening, speaking, writing, and literature.

E. Learning Story-Sharing Techniques

Share a story like <u>Little Red Riding Hood</u> by telling it with a flannelboard on which you mount (as you go along) geometric shapes representing story characters. Or better yet, ask a class member to prepare and share the story. Then, as follow-up, encourage the listeners to think up sounds and/or words they associate with each character. List these next to the names as follows:

        Wolf = woof woof
        Hunter = chop chop
        Red Riding Hood = la la la la la
        Mother = be good, be good, be good
        Grandma = snore snore

Now divide the listeners into five groups corresponding to the five major story characters. Retell the story (or instruct a class member to do so),pausing briefly whenever a character name is mentioned so that the appropriate listening group can interject the appropriate sound. This experience shows teachers firsthand how to create and orchestrate a sound-participation story with children.

F. Designing Listening Experiences with Stories

Divide the class into three-person task teams. Give each team three storybooks and a Task Sheet that states:

1. Each participant should read aloud to group members several beginning pages from one of the books. He or she should read expressively and display the pictures. After everyone has had a chance to read briefly, all should skim the unread portions of the books.

2. Using your text as a guide to the kinds of listening skills to be developed, design a literature-language experience based on one of the storybooks. Your experience should help children develop at least two different kinds of listening learnings. Outline your design as a flow chart, as we have done previously in class, noting both activity and language learning in a block within your flow chart.

3. Be prepared to share orally your design with the class and to explain why you sequenced it the way you did.

4. If you still have time while others are completing this task, design another literature-language experience, based on a second book.

G. Listening to and Creating a Drawing Story

Teachers who have experienced an approach are more likely to use it! That's the assumption on which many of the activities herein are predicated, especially this one. Share a drawing story from memory while sketching the accompanying drawing on the chalkboard. A classic is Carl Withers's <u>The Tale of a Black Cat</u> (Holt, Rinehart & Winston, 1966). Another is given in the Appendixes.

Follow up with individual or group composition during which pre- and in-service teachers themselves create original drawing stories to go along with this sketch:

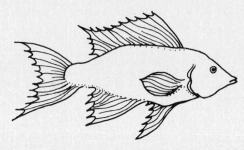

Encourage creators to share their stories in small presentational listening groups.

H. Trying Out Story-Sharing Techniques

Set out seven or eight small flannelboards in different areas of the room. Each board should have a packet of commercially produced flannel pieces for storytelling, such as those in the Fairy Story Collection marketed by Hammett. Have students in three- or four-person teams take turns sharing a story; each team should stay about ten minutes at a learning station and then move on to another station. The Task Sheet entitled "Using Flannelboards to Share Stories," found in Appendix B, can be distributed as a guide for the experience.

I. Thinking about Theory--Questions That Relate to the Chapter Forum.
1. According to Winn, why is it important that we teach listening in elementary grades? Which listening skills do you believe are most important? Give a rationale for your point of view.

2. According to Pearson and Fielding, what is necessary to improve children's listening comprehension.

3. What kinds of activities should be part of the teaching of listening in schools if children are to listen with comprehension? Describe ways to have children listen for main ideas and facts; describe ways to involve children in summarizing and sequencing as part of listening.

J. Reporting on Individual and Group Activities

Class members can present individual reports and/or panel discussions based on the following readings:

Boodt, Gloria. "Critical Listeners Become Critical Readers in Remedial Reading Class." <u>The Reading Teacher</u>, 37(January 1984): 390-394.

Choate, Joyce, and Thomas Rakes. "The Structured Listening Activity: A Model for Improving Listening Comprehension." The Reading Teacher, 41(November 1987): 194-199.

Coody, Betty. "Books for Reading Aloud." In Using Literature with Young Children, 3rd ed. Dubuque, Iowa: William C. Brown, 1983.

Fredericks, Anthony. "Mental Imagery Activities to Improve Comprehension." The Reading Teacher, 40(October 1986): 78-81.

Funk, Hal and Gary Funk. "Guidelines for Developing Listening Skills." The Reading Teacher, 42(May 1989): 660-663.

Hansen, Jane, and Donald Graves. "Do You Know What Backstrung Means?" The Reading Teacher, 39(April 1986): 807-812.

Pearson, David, and Linda Fielding. "Research Update: Listening Comprehension." Language Arts, 59(September 1982): 617-629.

Shoop, Mary. "InQuest: A Listening and Reading Comprehension Strategy." The Reading Teacher, 39(March 1986): 670-674.

Winn, Deanna. "Developing Listening Skills as a Part of the Curriculum." The Reading Teacher, 42(November 1988): 144-146.

Wright, Jane, and Lester Laminak. "First Graders Can Be Critical Listeners and Readers." Language Arts, 59(February 1982): 133-136.

IV. EXAMINATION QUESTIONS

A. Short Discussion Questions

1. Factors that determine how actively involved children become include (a) the physical design of classroom space, (b) the time of day, (c) the teacher, and (d) the children's age and level of self-control. Cite a specific example of each, and indicate how it is a determinant of listening involvement.

2. Educators speak of informational, critical, and appreciative listening. Using the data chart, describe for each kind of listening, an activity that is geared to developing a specific listening skill and write out the listening skill for which it is intended.

	Listening Activity	Specific Listening Skill
Informational Listening		
Critical Listening		
Appreciative Listening		

3. There are two kinds of critical listening. Distinguish between them by giving (a) specific listening learnings associated with each and (b) an activity to achieve each learning.

4. Describe what is meant by a <u>drawing story</u>, and tell the purpose for which it is used in elementary classrooms.

5. List one specific listening skill, and describe how it can be acquired through study in mathematics.

6. Describe how you could teach listening as part of work with computers.

7. Devise a check list for assessing critical listening skills.

B. Multiple-Choice Questions

1. Ernst has defined the nature of listening response. He proposes that
    a. Listening response is periodic if listeners are fully attending.
    b. Listening response is totally verbal.
    c. Listening response can be manifested in physical behavior.
    d. All of the above.

2. Research indicates that teachers tend to ask questions that
    a. Require the formulation of a judgment.
    b. Ask children to think creatively.
    c. Call for the giving of facts.
    d. Ask children to express their feelings.
    e. Make children formulate generalizations.

3. Listening in elementary schools can be made purpose-filled by
    a. Integrating listening learning into ongoing classroom activity.
    b. Teaching listening as part of literature study.
    c. Teaching listening as part of study in the content areas.
    d. a and b.
    e. a, b, and c.

4. Students listening to identify "snarl" and "purr" words are primarily engaged in
   a. Informational listening.
   b. Critical-analytical listening.
   c. Critical-judgmental listening.
   d. Appreciative listening.

5. Students listening to follow directions contained in an oral communication are primarily engaged in
   a. Informational listening.
   b. Critical-analytical listening.
   c. Critical-judgmental listening.
   d. Appreciative listening.

6. Students listening to classify story actions as good or bad, honest or dishonest, or fair or unfair are primarily engaged in
   a. Informational listening.
   b. Critical-analytical listening.
   c. Critical-judgmental listening.
   d. Appreciative listening.

7. Students distinguishing between fact and opinion are primarily engaged in
   a. Informational listening.
   b. Critical-analytical listening.
   c. Critical-judgmental listening.
   d. Appreciative listening.

8. Of the following sentences, which states an opinion rather than a fact?
   a. Mount Everest is the highest mountain in the world.
   b. The best thing to do is to decrease unemployment.
   c. Two centimeters of rain fell this afternoon.
   d. Potatoes are grown in Maine and Idaho.
   e. Morocco is in North Africa.

9. A television commercial states: "See this movie. It is the most creative film of the century in every aspect of its production!" This is an example of
   a. A glittering generality.
   b. The bandwagon effect.
   c. A testimonial.
   d. Deck stacking.
   e. A positive association.

10. A drawing story is one in which
    a. The listener draws a map in response to the story.
    b. The listener draws a picture in response to the story.
    c. The listener draws a graph in response to the story.
    d. The teller draws a picture as he or she orally shares the story.

11. A sound story is one in which
    a. The author has incorporated lots of alliterative effects.
    b. The author has incorporated lots of onomatopoeic effects.
    c. The listeners join in the storytelling by contributing appropriate sounds.
    d. The storyteller adds to the telling by making appropriate sounds.

12. Your book proposes that the best context(s) for developing children's ability to recall and respond to detail is (are)
    a. As students pursue cooperative work tasks.
    b. As students converse informally.
    c. As students respond to group presentations.
    d. All of the above.
    e. None of the above. The best context is through discrete lessons in which children talk about how to respond to detail.

13. Construction of time lines is a particularly appropriate way for students to
    a. Respond to story sequences.
    b. Listen for feelings.
    c. Listen for main ideas.
    d. Respond to "snarl" and "purr" words.
    e. Respond to story opinions.

14. Most educators recommend helping children first to
    a. Find the topic.
    b. Identify significant detail.
    c. Identify the main idea.
    d. Identify the author's point of view.

15. When a teacher says, "As I read this paragraph, I keep asking, 'How does this point relate to the one before?'" that teacher is
    a. Predicting.
    b. Modeling.
    c. Imagining.
    d. Setting the anticipatory set.

CHAPTER 5

ORAL COMMUNICATION--
SHARING STORIES AND POEMS THROUGH CREATIVE ACTIVITY

I.   CHAPTER THEMES--WHAT IS INTENDED

Chapter 5 provides ideas for involving children in creative oral expression.
It details ways to involve children in storytelling, creative drama, pantomime,
and drama festivals, and describes ways to use pictures, puppets, and objects
during story sharing. It also explains the whys and wherefores of choral
speaking and finger play.

II.   CHAPTER GOALS--WHAT IS TO BE LEARNED

Having read the chapter and completed the skill-building activities at the end
of each section, one should be able to state the following:

     I can describe ways to structure my class for sharing and can describe in
detail ways children can share stories with one another through pictures,
puppets, shapes and objects, pantomime, and dramatic playlets.

     I can describe ways to use creative drama in my classroom.

     I can study a poem and convert it into a choral-speaking activity
involving refrain, unison, line-a-child, sound group, round, and/or body chant.

     I can describe how to use finger play with primary-grade children and can
list the purposes served by such activity.

III.   IDEAS FOR CREATIVE ENCOUNTERS WITH LANGUAGE AND WITH INSTRUCTIONAL
       STRATEGIES

A.   Survey of Chapter 5

Ask students to brainstorm ideas that come to mind relative to the chapter
title and to record those ideas above the title web on the first page of the
chapter. Encourage students to survey the chapter headings and the summary
paragraph at the end of the chapter and to write questions or predictions to
guide their readings. Have them write these items beneath the title web from
lines attached to it. Remind students that in college texts there is often
space around the title where they can record "Getting Ready to Read" notes.
Tell them that they can use a similar "Getting Ready to Read" strategy as

children prepare to read a selection from a content-area textbook, except that
youngsters create their prereading webs on paper, not in their books. Use
Chapter 5, Master 1 to guide the prereading study when pursued as a class
activity, and record brainstormed ideas on it as students write their notes in
their books.

B. Presenting Stories

Perhaps the best way for prospective teachers to understand the diverse methods
available to elementary students who are sharing is to try out some of these
methods themselves. Prospective teachers can choose to present, either
individually or in groups, stories or poems of their own selection, using
presentational techniques and props that they devise themselves. Schedule
presentations (each to last about five minutes) during two or three drama
festival times--periods set aside for creative sharing. You may wish to have a
team draw up a duplicated program on the order of the one at the beginning of
Chapter 5 of Communication in Action, fourth edition. You may also wish to
suggest to participants that they listen for especially creative techniques
used by story sharers. At the end of each drama time, listeners can contribute
their findings. Ask the listeners to emphasize the good points of each
presentation, and suggest that children, too, learn much when emphasis is
placed on the positive rather than the negative.

C. Presenting Poems

1. Print out a Poetry Broadside Chart for the old favorite "The Animal Fair,"
or project Chapter 5, Master 3 while reciting the poem before the class.

THE ANIMAL FAIR

I went to the animal fair,
The birds and the beasts were there.
The big baboon by the light of the moon
Was combing his auburn hair.
The monkey he got drunk.
He stepped on the elephant's trunk.
The elephant sneezed
And fell on his knees,
And that was the end of the munk, the
munk, the munk.
And that was the end of the munk.

Ask the class to say the poem with you. Then divide the class into three
groups. Have one group begin by practicing the chant "munk, munk, munk" and
the second begin by practicing "munkety, munk, munkety, munk." Now bring in
the third group, which should speak the lines of the poem to the rhythm created
by the two chanting groups. You may want to help maintain the rhythm by
beating on a drum. The experience serves as a model for developing round
choral speaking in elementary schools.

2. Encourage class members to lead their colleagues in interpreting some of
the pieces found in Chapter 5 as choral speakings or readings. Encourage
others to locate poems that lend themselves easily to choral speaking. From

time to time, ask class members to share their findings with others by actually leading the group in a choral speaking.

3. Display Chapter 5, Master 2, and/or offer duplicated copies of Kate Greenaway's "Higgledy Piggledy" to pre- and in-service teachers who--in task groups--decide how to orchestrate the piece. Have groups take turns leading the entire class in its original version of the poem:

HIGGLEDY, PIGGLEDY

Higgledy, piggledy! See how they run!
Hopperty, popperty! What is the fun?
Has the sun or the moon tumbled into the sea?
What is the matter, now? Pray tell it me!
Higgledy, piggledy! How can I tell?
Hopperty, popperty! Hark to the bell!
The cats and the mice even scamper away:
Who can say what may not happen to-day?

Teachers may also follow up by considering what other forms of creative expression they could encourage through the Greenaway poem and go on to design a creative session based on it.

4. Whenever pre- or in-service teachers compose poetrylike pieces as a class, follow up by "doing" it as a choral reading or speaking so that participants begin to see how naturally choral speaking can fit into ongoing language experiences.

5. Share with students preparing to teach in the lower grades "Where Is Thumbkin?" as a finger play in which the students join in much the way kindergartners and first-graders would. Here are the words:

WHERE IS THUMBKIN?

Where is thumbkin? Where is thumbkin?	Hold both hands behind back.
Here I am. Here I am.	Bring out and hold up each thumb in turn.
How are you today, sir?	Shake one thumb at the other.
Very fine, I thank you.	Shake the opposite thumb in return.
Fly away.	Put one hand behind back.
Fly away.	Put other hand behind back.

(On successive repetitions, thumbkin becomes pointer, middle finger, ring finger, and pinkie.)

Ask students to prepare other finger plays and lead the class in doing them during other class sessions.

D. Analyzing Teaching

After students have read the opening teaching-in-action vignette, lead a discussion focusing on it. Questions to start include:

1. How did the teacher involve the children in prediction? Why do you think she did this?

2. Through what kind of activity did the children retell the story of the billy goats? From it, what do you learn about creative dramatics? How can the teacher get children involved in creative dramatics? What learnings can come from this activity?

3. What kinds of materials did the children and teacher use? What other materials could be used in a similar fashion?

4. In what ways was the children's transaction with Ox-Cart Man similar to their transaction with The Three Billy Goats Gruff? different from it?

5. What advantages do you see in this approach to teaching? What disadvantages? Do you want to teach this way? Why? Why not?

6. Do you remember the story Henny Penny, who thought the sky was falling? How could you structure a creative drama experience around it? How would you start? How would you continue? What materials would you use? What learnings would you hope as outcomes?

Use Chapter 4, Master 4 as follow-up. Students can complete the analysis guide on their own or in groups.

E. Analyzing Theory

After students have read the Forum in Chapter 5, ask them to sum up the purposes of creative oral expression in the classroom. Ask: What is the purpose of creative drama according to the Committee on the Role of Informal Drama in the Classroom? Do you agree? disagree? Why? How do Pamela Nelson and June Cottrell view drama?

F. Reporting on Individual and Group Activities

Topics for reporting can develop from these readings:

Bolton, G. "Changes in Thinking about Drama in Education." Theory into Practice, 24(Summer 1985): 151-157.

Cowen, John. Teaching Reading through the Arts. Newark, Del.: International Reading Association, 1983.

Edmiston, Brian, et al. "Empowering Readers and Writers through Drama: Narrative Theater." Language Arts, 64(February 1987): 219-228.

Greene, Ellin. "A Peculiar Understanding: Re-creating the Literary Fairy Tale." The Horn Book, 59(June 1983): 270-278, 378.

Heathcote, Dorothy. "Learning, Knowing, and Languaging in Drama." Language Arts, 60(September 1983): 695-696.

Kukla, Kaila. "David Booth: Drama as a Way of Knowing." Language Arts, 64(January 1987): 73-78.

Morgan, Norah, and Juliana Saxton. "Enriching Language through Drama." Language Arts, 65(January 1988): 34-40.

Nelson, Olga. "Storytelling: Language Experience for Meaning Making." The Reading Teacher, 42(February 1989): 386-391.

Nelson, Pamela. "Drama, Doorway to the Past." Language Arts, 65(January 1988): 20-25.

Nessel, Denise. "Storytelling in the Reading Program." The Reading Teacher, 38(January 1985): 378-381.

O'Neill, Cecily. "Dialogue and Drama: The Transformation of Events, Ideas, and Teacher." Language Arts, 66(February 1989): 147-159.

Ross, Cameron. "Drama Ground: Premises and Promises." Language Arts, 65(January 1988): 41-45.

San Jose, Christine. "Story Drama in the Content Areas." Language Arts, 65(January 1988): 26-33.

Schwartz, Marni. "Connecting to Language through Story." Language Arts, 64 (October 1987): 603-610.

Shuy, Roger. "Research Currents: Dialogue as the Heart of Learning." Language Arts, 64(December 1987): 890-897.

Verriour, Patrick. "This is Drama: The Play Beyond the Play." Language Arts, 66(March 1989): 276-286.

Wagner, Betty Jane. "Elevating the Written Word through the Spoken: Dorothy Heathcoate and a Group of 9-13-Year-Olds as Monks." Theory into Practice, 24(Summer 1985): 166-172.

_____. "Research Currents: Does Classroom Drama Affect the Arts of Language?" Language Arts, 65(January 1988): 46-55.

IV. EXAMINATION QUESTIONS

A. Short Discussion Questions

1. Define creative drama. Then describe two ways to use it in the classroom.

2. a. Why is story retelling important?
   b. How should the teacher use story retelling in the primary grades?

3. Older children especially should be asked to participate in orchestrating a choral speaking. Outline five kinds of questions students should consider in deciding how to "do" a particular piece.

B. Multiple-Choice Questions

1. Which of the following represents an *unwise* use of choral speaking?
   a. Children spontaneously chorus together pieces they have written.
   b. Children interpret a poem to determine how to chorus it.
   c. Children discover things about vocal interpretation of punctuation through choral speaking.
   d. Children expand choral speaking into spontaneous dramatizations.
   e. Children memorize and perform lengthy pieces for assembly presentation.

2. Finger play has a significant role in language arts programs for
   a. Children in the elementary grades K-6.
   b. Young children in grades K-1.
   c. Middle-graders (grades 2-4).
   d. Upper-graders (grade 5-6).

3. A basic principle inherent in the design of sharing sessions in elementary schools is that
   a. Dramatization should be a magnificent production, with elaborate props and scenery.
   b. Children should memorize lines till they know them completely.
   c. Students should be given a letter grade on their sharings to encourage effort.
   d. Sharing should be relatively informal.
   e. Children should be cautioned about "hamming it up" as they share.

4. Which of the following is an effective way to use puppets in elementary classrooms?
   a. Do little preparatory work with sounds and actions so that students can react with complete spontaneity.
   b. Suggest that each child manipulate just one puppet so that he or she can interpret the action fully.
   c. Suggest that children learn their lines by heart so that they will have confidence in the presentation.
   d. Involve many puppets in each show to ensure much dramatic appeal and action.
   e. All of the above.

5. Which of the following is an effective way to start pantomime activity?
   a. As a total class activity so that children will feel freer about expressing.
   b. As an individual activity so that children's expression will be more creative.
   c. As a small-group activity so that children will learn to cooperate with one another.

6. Why are stories ideal material to share?
   a. Children love to hear stories and quickly develop an interest in sharing.
   b. Stories are a simple introduction to the oral sequencing of ideas.
   c. With stories, it is relatively easy to integrate oral expression with listening and reading.
   d. The action in stories makes for expressive sharing.
   e. All of the above are true.

7. According to Dorothy Heathcote, which of the following are important principles underlying the use of creative drama in classrooms?
   a. Creative drama should be used in relation to factual material.
   b. The teacher should view his/her role in classroom drama as journeymaker.
   c. The teacher should press students to get at the meanings behind the material they are studying.
   d. The teacher should pose the problem situation.
   e. All of the above are important.

CHAPTER 6

ORAL COMMUNICATION--
SHARING IDEAS THROUGH CONVERSING AND REPORTING

I. CHAPTER THEMES--WHAT IS INTENDED

Chapter 6 provides background on the function of language and suggestions on ways to help children use oral language as they converse informally and report findings to one another. It also describes ways to build skills important in gathering ideas for sharing, such as collecting data, noting, and jotting down. Although the emphasis in this latter section is on researching ideas preparatory to oral reporting and discussing, the skills described apply to written expression as well.

II. CHAPTER GOALS--WHAT IS TO BE LEARNED

Having read the chapter, one should be able to state:

I can explain the functions for which people use language, according to the construct set forth by Michael Halliday; I can describe ways to structure classroom interaction so that children use language to serve a full range of language functions.

I can list key conversational skills to be acquired and can structure classroom sequences that lead to the development of these skills. I can explain a number of grouping schemes that encourage social interaction.

I can describe ways to encourage courteous communication.

I can design lesson sequences that involve children with information-gathering tasks preparatory to classroom reporting and discussing. I can explain how students in elementary grades can be involved in locating information and in selecting and summarizing it for presentation.

I can explain ways to help children use their voices and bodies effectively during oral sharing.

I can design classroom sequences that include panels, individual reports, and small feedback groups (where applicable).

I can list several basic guidelines for building an assessment program and can create a check list of skills to use in evaluating children's growth in oral-communication and study skills.

III. IDEAS FOR CREATIVE ENCOUNTERS WITH LANGUAGE AND WITH INSTRUCTIONAL
      STRATEGIES

A. Survey of Chapter 6

Ask students to brainstorm ideas that come to mind relative to the chapter
title and to record those ideas above the title web on the first page of the
chapter. Encourage students to survey the chapter headings and the summary
paragraph at the end of the chapter and to write questions or predictions to
guide their reading. Have them write these items beneath the title web from
lines attached to it. Remind students that in college texts there is often
space around the title where they can record "Getting Ready to Read" notes.
Tell them that they can use a similar "Getting Ready to Read" strategy as
children prepare to read a selection from a content-area textbook, except that
youngsters create their prereading webs on paper, not in their books. Use
Chapter 6, Master 1 to guide the prereading study when pursued as a class
activity, and record brainstormed ideas on it as students write their notes in
their books.

B. Analyzing Teaching

Here are some general questions to guide readers' interpretation of the opening
Teaching-in-Action episode. You may duplicate them for use by small discussion
groups and then schedule a reporting time so that the groups can share their
thoughts with the entire class.

1. Describe the organization of an Idea Fair. What do you feel are the
purposes served by Mr. Bruce's Fair?

2. What are the advantages of the Fair format over the typical approach in
which each child presents a report individually and serially to the entire
class? What are the disadvantages?

3. Explain the meaning of the terms <u>illustrated reporting</u>, <u>revolving groups</u>,
and <u>seminar</u>.

4. How did Mr. Bruce structure the informal give-and-take of discussion into
his teaching sequence? What does this imply about the teaching of discussion
skills and the teaching of reporting skills?

5. How did Mr. Bruce help children prepare for oral reporting and discussion?
What does this imply about the way a teacher in general must teach such skills?

6. Do you think an Idea Fair would work in the early primary grades? How
might you adapt this way of teaching for use with younger children? for use
with story content rather than subject-matter content?

Use Chapter 6, Master 2 as follow-up. Students can complete the analysis guide
on their own or in groups.

C. Analyzing Theory

Use these questions in relation to the Forum on page 177 of the text and the section that explains Michael Halliday's ideas on the functions of language, pages 175-179.

1. What is dialogue? Why is dialogue important? How can we get dialogue back into the classroom? Why do some teachers fear dialogue in their classrooms?

2. What are the functions for which we use language, according to Michael Halliday? How can the teacher structure classroom social interaction so that youngsters use language to serve these functions?

D. Sharing Information

1. Sharing information can be a natural part of ongoing activity in college language arts courses as well as in elementary classrooms. Each chapter of this guide provides topics for individual or group reporting that can be sandwiched into class sessions. As pre- and in-service teachers prepare for reporting, suggest that they utilize interesting visuals to heighten impact.

2. Likewise, when students read in preparation for seminar-type sessions, such as that on dialectally different children in Chapter 13, suggest they prepare Note Cards of important ideas and use them as sources of data during discussion.

3. Suggest that students maintain a Jotting Book of specific teaching ideas encountered during class sessions, ideas encountered in reading, and original extensions of ideas read and heard. Periodically ask students to share innovative teaching ideas from their Jotting Books.

E. Systematic Noting

1. To show teachers the value of data-retrieval charting as a note-taking device, ask them to complete a chart (like the following one) as they read their text. Information for the chart is found on pages 193-195 of Communication in Action, fourth edition.

DATA CHART OF FORMATS FOR REPORTING

	Description of Format	Advantages of Format	Limitations, if Any
Small Feedback Group			
Panel Presentation			
Individual Report			

2. Ask college students in work teams to construct a data-retrieval chart to use in gathering data from another subtopic included in Chapter 6. Possible subtopics include grouping schemes for classroom conversations; teaching children to take notes; learning to record through taping, sketching, and photographing; and Halliday's language functions.

F. Generating Questions

Ask college students to read a content-area selection and to devise a series of questions based on it to lead children into higher-order thinking. Chapter 6, Master 3 is a guide for college students--functioning in task groups--to use to complete this task.

G. Analyzing Data-Collection Devices

Project the outline from Communication in Action that is available as Chapter 6, Master 4 of this guide. Ask college students, working in pairs, to translate the outline first into a data web and then into a data chart. Ask them to compare and contrast the three organizational frameworks for note taking and to decide which one is best for their own use.

H. Reporting on Individual and Group Activity

Related readings for reporting include the following:

Adams, Anthony. "Talk and Learning in the Classroom: An Interview with Anthony Adams." Language Arts, 61(February 1984): 119-124.

Comber, Barbara. "Celebrating and Analyzing Successful Teaching." Language Arts, 64(February 1987): 182-195.

Eller, Rebecca. "Johnny Can't Talk Either: The Perpetuation of the Deficit Theory in Classrooms." The Reading Teacher, 42(May 1989): 670-673.

Fine, Michelle. "Silencing in Public Schools." Language Arts, 64(February 1987): 157-174.

Flood, James, and Diane Lapp. "Conceptual Mapping Strategies for Understanding Informational Texts." The Reading Teacher, 41(April 1988): 780-783.

Hennings, Dorothy Grant. "A Writing Approach to Reading Comprehension." Language Arts, 59(January 1982): 8-17.

Holbrook, Hilary. "ERIC/RCS Report: The Quiet Student in Your Classroom." Language Arts, 64(September 1987): 554-557.

Lindfors, Judith Wells. "From 'Talking Together' to 'Being Together in Talk.'" Language Arts, 65(February 1988): 135-141.

McKenzie, Gary. "Data Charts: A Crutch for Helping Pupils Organize Reports." Language Arts, 56(October 1978): 784-788.

Schmidt, Marion. "The Shape of Content: Four Semantic Map Structures for Expository Paragraphs." The Reading Teacher, 40(October 1986): 113-117.

Wilekinson, Louise. "Research Currents: Peer Group Talk in Elementary School." Language Arts, (February 1984): 164-169.

Wray, David. "Teaching Information Skills in the U.K. Elementary School." The Reading Teacher, 41(February 1988): 520-525.

IV. EXAMINATION QUESTIONS

A. Short Discussion Questions

1. Briefly describe how you would use each of the following in a language arts program:
    a. Note Cards.
    b. Jotting Books.
    c. Data charts.
    d. Revolving groups.
    e. Task groups.

2. Create a data chart in which you distinguish among the small feedback group, the panel presentation, and the individual report. On the chart, include a description and the advantages of each of these things.

3. Describe the functions for which people use language, and explain ways to encourage children to use language in the classroom to serve those functions.

B. Multiple-Choice Question

1. You are planning an Idea Fair. Of the following, which would you be <u>least</u> likely to use a part of your Idea Fair?
    a. Revolving groups.
    b. Discussion.
    c. Illustrated reporting.
    d. Teacher lecture.

2. To make an Idea Fair successful, there must be
    a. A thorough investigation of topics by students.
    b. A use of visuals as a sharing device.
    c. Simultaneous instruction by the teacher in how to handle data and organize them for presentation.
    d. All of the above.
    e. a and b.

3. Of the following, which is the best context for teaching information-gathering skills?
    a. As part of natural and social science units.
    b. As part of story times.
    c. As part of discrete language arts lessons.
    d. Through use of the language arts text in which such skill are described in detail.

4. An advantage of Jotting Books over Note Cards is that Jotting Books are
    a. Cumulative.
    b. Less organized.
    c. Less useful.
    d. Less handy.

5. Data charts are particularly useful when students
    a. Must take notes from several references.
    b. Must organize notes based on subtopics they have brainstormed together.
    c. Must see a need for data collection, preparatory to oral or written reporting.
    d. All of the above.

6. Why should teachers encourage the use of visuals in reporting?
    a. Visuals hold listeners' attention.
    b. Visuals serve as organizing notes for a speaker.
    c. Students who use visuals are learning the skills of forceful communication.
    d. All of the above.
    e. a and b.

7. Of the following, which is an advantage of small feedback groups?
    a. Students learn to report to larger audiences.
    b. Listeners must learn not to respond.
    c. Students must repeat their reports.
    d. All of the above.
    e. None of the above.

8. Displaying a chart with items like "Wait your turn" or "Say please" is set forth in your text as
   a. A technique that will probably result in few behavioral changes.
   b. A relatively productive way of teaching courtesy associated with the communication process.
   c. Probably the single most important strategy for teaching courteous listening and speaking.

9. According to Halliday, which language function is the last to emerge?
   a. Heuristic.
   b. Imaginative.
   c. Informative.
   d. Regulatory.
   e. Instrumental.

10. According to Halliday, young children learn to use language through
    a. Imitation.
    b. Interaction.
    c. Direct instruction.
    d. Indirect instruction.

CHAPTER 7

THINKING OUT LOUD--
TALKING, LISTENING, WRITING, AND READING TOGETHER

I. CHAPTER THEMES--WHAT IS INTENDED

Chapter 7 presents ways of using firsthand experiences, perceptions derived
from all the senses, brainstorming, and value considerations to trigger
children to think, talk, write, and read. The result is a program in which
children meet the language arts as an integrated whole and often as part of
content-area study; it is a program in which children have the opportunity to
think and talk about a variety of ideas.

II. CHAPTER GOALS--WHAT IS TO BE LEARNED

Having read the chapter, one should be able to state the following:

    I can design experiences in which children talk, write, and read, based on
classroom activity and on excursions into the larger world.

    I can structure experiences in which children feel with all their senses--
taste, touch, smell, sight, and hearing--and us these feelings as a base for
group talking, writing, and reading.

    I can describe characteristics of brainstorming and can ask questions that
trigger many ideas and words.

    I can design activities in which students together make value judgments
about actions, support their judgments with reasons, and then write and read.
I can set these activities on paper in the form of "talk tracks."

III. IDEAS FOR CREATIVE ENCOUNTERS WITH LANGUAGE AND WITH INSTRUCTIONAL
      STRATEGIES

A. Survey of Chapter 7

Ask students to brainstorm ideas that come to mind relative to the chapter
title and to record those ideas above the title web on the first page of the
chapter. Encourage students to survey the chapter headings and the summary
paragraph at the end of the chapter and to write questions or predictions to
guide their reading. Have them write these items beneath the title web from
lines attached to it. Remind students that in college texts there is often

61

space around the title where they can record "Getting Ready to Read" notes. Tell them that they can use a similar "Getting Ready to Read" strategy as children prepare to read a selection from a content-area textbook, except that youngsters create their prereading webs on paper, not in their books. Use Chapter 7, Master 1 to guide the prereading study when pursued as a class activity, and record brainstormed ideas on it as students write their notes in their books.

B. Valuing Together--A Group Experience

Pre- and in-service teachers need to experience firsthand some of the instructional strategies through which they can guide children in making value judgments that can be supported with reasons. You can involve teachers in a valuing-together session much on the order of The Lorax episode recounted in Chapter 7 of the text. This provides participants with a model that they can use to design further valuing sessions for talking and writing. It also lays the foundation for comparative and creative sessions to follow.

    You can use The Five Chinese Brothers by Claire Bishop (Coward, 1938) as the content for a college-level values-clarification experience. Introduce the book either by reading it aloud or by showing the Weston Woods film. Ask the participants to listen in order to identify those actions committed in the story which were wrong. After the listening, ask volunteers to record on the board the specific wrong acts and to suggest why each one was wrong. Then ask participants individually to copy the list of wrong acts onto the rungs of a ladder on which the most evil act is recorded on the uppermost rung, the least evil on the bottom rung, and the other acts in between in order of wrongness.

    Next, have participants form five-person teams. Tell teams that by discussing, compromising, and voting, each should come to a group rank-ordering of the acts--a rank ordering team members should be prepared to defend rationally. Teams should record their orderings on a chalkboard chart and explain in a follow-up discussion the reason that they feel their orderings are justifiable. In leading the class follow-up discussion, help participants identify those basic beliefs they hold which underlie their decision making-- beliefs such as "The reason a bad act is committed should be taken into account in meting out punishment" and "People should keep their end of an agreement." A class scribe can record these basic beliefs.

    Now instruct the original five-person teams to reconvene, this time to select one of the basic beliefs recorded by the scribe and to share specific examples from their own experience that clarify why that belief is fundamental and worthy. Have each team vote on the "best" example from those offered by team members and write it up in brief (on large charting paper) beneath the statement of belief for which it is an example. Post the charts on the wall of the classroom; team members should then circulate informally to read other teams' charts.

C. Analyzing Together

1. Follow the class valuing-together session with an analytical session in which participants identify critical aspects, either as a class or in small

groups. Key questions, which could be distributed in the form of a Task Sheet, can include the following:
   a.   What was the sequence of instructional events? What purpose did each event serve in the total lesson?
   b.   What instructional strategies do we find in both the class experience with The Five Chinese Brothers and in The Lorax episode?
        (1) How does each start?
        (2) How is rank-ordering used? How is voting used?
        (3) How do small-group and class discussions feed into each other?
   c.   At what grade level does such activity become feasible? Refer to the material from Piaget on the development of judgmental skills as set forth in Chapter 2.
   d.   How would The Five Chinese Brothers activity experienced in class have to be modified for use with elementary students?
   e.   What kinds of value judgments should primary students be guided to make?
   f.   What kinds of listening are a part of such valuing-together times?

2.   In groups, class members can analyze the brainstorming experience based on The Biggest House in the World, found on pages 212-216 of their text. Questions to guide the analysis can be duplicated and distributed as a Task Sheet:
   a.   What are the assumptions that this teacher holds about the nature of instruction and language learning?
   b.   What would this teacher's plans probably have looked like? Draw a probable schematic.
   c.   What was the teacher's function in this teaching-learning situation?
   d.   Why did the teacher have
        (1) The children listen to the Lionni story about the snail?
        (2) The children handle the real mollusk?
        (3) One youngster record brainstormed words?
        (4) The children compose the diamante together?
        (5) The children interpret their group writing as a choral speaking?
   e.   Of all the teaching episodes you have read about in your text or experienced directly in class, which one is structurally most similar to this one?

3.   As an alternative to the previous activity, analyze The Lorax episode in Chapter 7. Use Chapter 7, Master 2 as the base of the discussion.

D.   Designing Together

You may decide to give teachers time in class to design teaching-learning sequences through which children can brainstorm and/or ponder together. Either suggest to participants that each bring to class three picture storybooks or you bring enough basal readers so that each three-person team receives one. The advantage of your bringing basal readers is that teachers realize that these approaches can be applied even with content from basal reading books. During the session, have teams select one story and create a learning experience that is based on that content and includes some activity with brainstorming and/or valuing. Provide participants with large charting paper on which to record their original designs. Post the designs around the room, and allow time for walking around to peruse other teams' designs and for talking as a class about the strengths of the proposed designs.

E. Sharing Together

Ask teachers and teachers-in-training who are currently working with children to try brainstorming and valuing in their classes. Set aside--especially in seminars with teachers-in-training--time for sharing designs and results, for evaluating successes, and for considering ways in which plans can be modified for use in particular classroom situations.

F. Talking Together

Encourage college students to brainstorm ways of using brainstorming. Place the word brainstorming at the center of a weblike graphic, as in Chapter 7, Master 3. As students suggest creative possibilities, add them directly to the projected transparency. Generalize about the uses of brainstorming in elementary classrooms.

G. Reporting on Individual and Group Activities

Individual reports and panel discussions can develop from the following independent readings.

Allen, Elizabeth, et al. "Using Language Experience to ALERT Pupils' Critical Thinking Skills." The Reading Teacher, 41(May 1988): 904-910.

Avery, Carol. "First Grade Thinkers Becoming Literate." Language Arts, 64(October 1987): 611-618.

Barrs, Myra. "Voice and Role in Reading and Writing." Language Arts, 64(February 1987): 207-218.

Comber, Barbara. "Any Questions? Any Problems? Inviting Children's Questions and Requests for Help." Language Arts, 65(February 1988): 147-153.

Genishi, Celia, et al. "Research Currents: Dialogue as a Context for Teaching and Learning." Language Arts, 65(February 1988): 182-191.

Golub, Jeff. Activities to Promote Critical Thinking. Urbana, Ill: National Council of Teachers of English, 1986.

Heller, Mary. "Comprehending and Composing through Language Experience." The Reading Teacher, 42(November 1988): 130-135.

Johnson, Dale, et al. "Semantic Mapping." The Reading Teacher, 39(April 1986):778-783.

Madden, Lowell. "Do Teachers Communicate with Their Students as if They Were Dogs?" Language Arts, 65(February 1988): 142-146.

McMillan, Merna, and Lance Gentile. "Children's Literature: Teaching Critical Thinking and Ethics." The Reading Teacher, 41(May 1988): 142-146.

Smith, Carl. "Prompting Critical Thinking." The Reading Teacher, 42(February 1989): 424.

Stahl, Steven and Sandra Vancil. "Discussion Is What Makes Semantic Maps Work in Vocabulary Instruction." The Reading Teacher, 40(October 1986): 62-67.

H. Film Viewing

The following films, all available from Weston Woods, can be used as the content for value discussions with teachers and teachers-in-training: All Gold Canyon (running time, 21 minutes); The Giants (running time, 10 minutes); Mr. Koumal (a series of 9 vignettes, each with a running time of 1 1/2--2 1/2 minutes). Or teachers can ponder how they could use any one of the films as content for an elementary values lesson and project a sequence of activities and questions to use with each.

Still another excellent film series to use for values decision making with pre- and in-service teachers is the National Geographic Society's Decades of Decision: The American Revolution. Favorite titles of this instructor include Equally Free, Mary Kate's War, and King's Mountain.

 IV. EXAMINATION QUESTIONS

A. Short Discussion Questions

1. Open your text to the teaching episode with Ms. Donovan and the billy goat.
    a. Identify three basic assumptions about instruction and language learning inherent in Ms. Donovan's design.
    b. Diagram in flow-chart style Ms. Donovan' probable plans for the episode.
    c. Explain why Ms. Donovan did each of the following:
        (1) Asked children to volunteer specific reasons for liking Billy.
        (2) Took children to the farm in the first place.
        (3) Recorded the story for the children on charting paper.

2. The text suggests that children should think about what they are tasting, touching, smelling, seeing, and hearing. Describe an activity in which you could involve children so that they think about impressions received via all five senses.

3. Assume you are guiding children in brainstorming words and ideas about Halloween. List five specific questions you can ask that could conceivably trigger a stream of words and phrases.

4. Voting, rank-ordering, and defending a rank-ordering are specific strategies to get students involved in thinking and talking together. For each of these strategies, explain what purpose is served within a pondering-together time.

5. Familiar fairy tales can serve as the content for a pondering-together time. Plan a sequence of steps for involving students in pondering right and wrong in a story such as The Three Bears, Hansel and Gretal, The Little Red Hen, Jack and the Bean Stalk, or any other tale you remember. If you wish, you may diagram the steps in the lesson as a talk track.

6. Among the reasons for following discussions with group composing are:
    a. Teachers can discover whether participants have followed the
        progression of ideas discussed.
    b. Discussion provides ideas for writing.
    c. Writing provide a review of ideas discussed.
    d. Children can learn writing skills as part of ongoing class activity.
    Rank-order the four purposes from most to least significant. Then write a
    paragraph justifying your ordering. (<u>Note to evaluator</u>: any rank-
    ordering is plausible since the essence of the answer lies in the
    explanatory paragraph.

B. Multiple-Choice Questions

1. At what grade level or levels is writing together a useful
    teaching/learning strategy?
    a. In grades K-1.
    b. In grades K-3.
    c. In grades 4-6.
    d. In all elementary grades.

2. Of the following statements about brainstorming, which one is <u>least</u>
    accurate?
    a. Brainstorming should always flow out of firsthand immediate
        experience.
    b. All contributions should be accepted equally.
    c. All contributions should be recorded prominently.
    d. Each student should contribute whatever ideas or words come to mind.

3. What is the structure of a diamante?
    a. 3 lines with a total of 17 syllables.
    b. 3 lines based on parts of speech.
    c. 5 lines with a total of 22 syllables.
    d. 5 lines based on parts of speech.
    e. 7 lines with a total of 34 syllables.
    f. 7 lines based on parts of speech.

4. The purpose of brainstorming as an instructional strategy is to
    a. Provide words and ideas for writing.
    b. Encourage thinking.
    c. Build vocabulary.
    d. All of the above.

5. Children playing with word pairs such as <u>bright/dull</u> and <u>rough/smooth</u> are
    developing an understanding of
    a. Homographs.
    b. Homophones.
    c. Homonyms.
    d. Synonyms.
    e. Antonyms.

6. Which of the following best describes current ideas about critical thinking?
   a. There is 100 percent agreement about what critical thinking is.
   b. There is close to 100 percent agreement about what critical thinking is.
   c. There is some disagreement about what critical thinking is.
   d. There is complete disagreement about what critical thinking is.

7. Taba is well known for her work with
   a. Values.
   b. Questioning patterns.
   c. Listening skills.
   d. Informal conversations.
   e. All of the above.

8. When children ponder together, they should
   a. Arrive at the same opinion.
   b. Have content to ponder and discuss.
   c. Learn skills separate from work with literature and the content areas.
   d. Begin with higher-level thinking tasks.
   e. All of the above.

9. In his advocacy of judgmental voting, Sidney Simon proposes
   a. Use of secret ballots tallied by a student committee.
   b. Use of paper ballots tallied by the teacher.
   c. Voting only by those who have contributed to the prior talk session.
   d. Verbal aye-nay votes as the activity proceeds.
   e. Different nonverbal signals by arms and hands.

10. As set forth in the text, "talking about" is essentially
    a. A skill to be learned.
    b. An attitude to be learned.
    c. Content to be learned.
    d. An interest to be developed.
    e. An appreciation to be acquired and refined.

CHAPTER 8

WRITING AS IDEA MAKING--THOUGHT IN ACTION

I.   CHAPTER THEMES--WHAT IS INTENDED

Chapter 8 describes the writing development of young children and the nature of
creativity. It then describes specific ways of guiding children as they create
fresh ideas, use language in creative ways, and relate words and visual images
in novel patterns. Final sections provide ideas for personal writing.

II.   CHAPTER GOALS--WHAT IS TO BE LEARNED

Having read the chapter and completed the skill-building activities at the end
of each section, one should be able to state the following:

     I can explain the writing development of young children and describe ways
to involve children naturally in writing.

     I can explain the complexity of the creative act, and I recognize the
importance of involving children in creative thinking and writing.

     I can describe several ways to stretch children's imagination so that
they produce uncommon ideas; I can create additional mind-stretching activities
along the same lines.

     I can involve children firsthand in the elements of personification,
metaphor, and simile without stressing knowledge of terminology.

     I can help children create writing that paints pictures through words,
that has a nice ring to it, and that gains impact from unique sound-meaning
relationships.

     I can describe many forms for creative expression, including free
thought, haiku, tanka, senryu, cinquain, sound plays, rhyming plays, couplets,
limericks, figured verse, and acrostics. I enjoy using these forms in writing.

     I can guide children in producing letters, diaries, and reports that
reflect creativity.

69

III. IDEAS FOR CREATIVE ENCOUNTERS WITH LANGUAGE AND WITH
      INSTRUCTIONAL STRATEGIES

A. Survey of Chapter 8

Ask students to think about the title of the chapter, brainstorm ideas relative
to it, and record those ideas on the title web on the first page of the
chapter. Encourage students also to survey the chapter headings and the
summary paragraph at the end of the chapter and to write questions or
predictions to guide their reading. Have them note these items beneath the
title web from lines attached to it. Remind students that in college texts
there is often space around the title where they can record "Getting Ready to
Read" notes in the same way. Tell them that they can use a similar "Getting
Ready to Read" strategy with children as they prepare to read a selection from
a content-area textbook. Use Chapter 8, Master 1 to guide the prereading study
when done as a class activity.

B. Analysis of Teaching-in-Action Vignette--"Journals, Ideas Clusters, and
    Other Ways to Make Ideas"

Involve students in an analysis of the series of activities described in the
vignette at the opening of the chapter. About each activity, ask these
questions: What is this teacher doing at this point? Why is she doing this?
What does she hope to achieve? Chapter 8, Master 2 can serve as a guide for
the session. Make a copy from the master so that each student has a copy.
Project the master as a transparency during the discussion, with students
coming forward to add points to it in summary fashion as they take notes on
their own copies.

C. Discussion of Dialogue Journals

If students have been dialoguing with you in journals as suggested in the
introduction to this guide, involve them in a discussion of the advantages and
disadvantages of this teaching technique. Use Chapter 8, Master 3 as a
discussion guide.

D. Idea Clustering--A Way of Making Ideas

1. You may wish to model idea clustering and drafting based on a cluster. To
do this, simply distribute construction paper and crayons, stand at the board
as Ms. Chou did, and tell your college students something like this:

> Driving to the college this morning in the rain, I was thinking about the
> rain and the traffic. I was feeling frustrated about it all and thought
> I would like to write out my frustrations. When I feel this way, I put
> the topic I am thinking about in the middle of a piece of paper and
> circle it. [Demonstrate on the board by writing <u>driving to work on a</u>
> <u>rainy day</u>.] To my topic words, I add words that come to mind.
> [Demonstrate by connecting words to the topic words: <u>traffic, fast cars,</u>
> <u>trucks throwing water at my windshield, danger, skidding</u>.]
> Now ask students to help you by providing other related words. Tell them
> to idea-doodle based on your topic, making their own idea clusters that

70

have words of their own and some of your words. Encourage students to help you find several beginning sentences or lines to get you started writing.

2. As follow-up, structure a writing workshop. Students may do any one of the following:

o Write individually about "Driving to Work on a Rainy Day," using words from the idea cluster and even starting with one of the brainstormed beginnings.

o Write on that topic in three-person teams, using words from the idea cluster.

o Create an original idea cluster on a topic of their own choosing or on one of these--Life's Problems," "The Opposite Sex," "After College," or "Where I Want to Be"--and then write something based on the cluster.

E. Creative Writing Workshops

Pre- and in-service teachers get a clearer conception of the nature of the creative act by becoming directly involved in the creation of ideas and of patterns for expressing ideas during creative writing workshops scheduled in language arts methods courses. During workshop sessions, teachers create together, guided at first by questions projected by the college instructor.

1. Stretching ideas through comparisons. A creative workshop can begin by brainstorming, starting with the trigger word war (which is good for the college level because of related abstractions). Ask: What words describe war? What words are associated with the actions of war? What words are associated with our feelings about war? A class scribe should record idea words on the board or a chart.

   Then go on saying: I could say that war is an octopus that reaches out to strangle life. What else is war like? As participants propose such things as monsters, dragons, devils, fire, storms, sharks, demons, and steamrollers, ask them to explain how the thing is like war. The object is to get the brainstormers to produce lengthier phrases replete with descriptors. Next, ask: If war were one of these things and could talk, what would it say? Have the scribe record these ideas, too. Then ask participants to identify the analogy they think is best, and guide them in the creation of a "war thought." You might suggest a simple beginning, such as "War is . . ." and ask participants to try out arrangements of words to select a combination that projects a clear picture "soundfully." Record the class product on charting paper.

   As follow-up, suggest that participants individually record the kinds of questions you asked to trigger words and ideas and the steps in the sequence they just experienced. Suggest that they think about words other than war that might be more appropriate to use as "idea triggers" in elementary classrooms.

2. Group composing. Some interesting results can be triggered by asking participants who have done some preliminary group brainstorming and writing to tear a piece of paper into four segments. On the first segment, they should record any three random thoughts that come to mind when they think of autumn (or whatever season it is); on the second, any three random thoughts triggered by the word blue; on the third, any three thoughts triggered by love; and on

the last, any three thoughts triggered by <u>loneliness</u>. The only ground rule is to have no names on the papers. When all are finished, half the autumn slips should be folded and passed to a student leader, with the remaining autumn slips going to a second student. The same should be done with the other slips, so that eight participants will be holding a pile of slips on the same topic. These eight then become the hub of student writing groups, who choose and order items from the slips, add other thoughts, and compose a free thought that begins:

Autumn (blue, love, loneliness) is _____

_____

_____

3. <u>A branching haiku</u>. You can use almost any of the ideas on pages 279-281 of the text with college students to guide them in group creation of a haiku moment. One activity that has proved most successful with this instructor is to display a large, graceful branch, swinging it back and forth in the air, and to ask participants to think of action and describing words that come to mind. Suggest that the class put some of the words together to express a fleeting thought about the branch in only seventeen syllables, broken into three lines (5-7-5). At the college level this can be done completely as an oral activity, with participants holding the haiku moment in their minds as they try out different combinations of words and sounds to produce a striking thought. If you record the thought, help participants choose the right combination of colons, dashes, commas, and periods to heighten the effect.

4. <u>Squiggling together</u>. Some direct involvement with figure poems makes pre- and in-service teachers more aware of the potential for creative expression inherent in this form. For this purpose, duplicate and distribute one of these squiggles and brainstorm with the class the things it could represent.

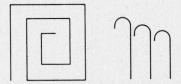

To trigger a multitude of thoughts, suggest that students examine it from many different directions, even climbing inside and looking out! Students should finally compromise by choosing one of the suggestions. Then together they should create lines that describe the chosen object and record those on the line of the squiggle. As follow-up, college-level students can do the following:
   a. In groups, compose additional lines based on other suggestions and record them as figure poems.
   b. Individually concoct additional squiggles to trigger thinking at the elementary level.

72

c. Individually write such words as <u>upstairs</u>, <u>cracked</u>, and <u>tiny</u> to show meaning.

d. Individually create an original squiggle thought.

5. <u>Hyperboling</u>. college students enjoy hyperboles. Do one as a class to introduce the form. Start by saying: I am so tiny that a mite is large compared to me. Ask students to try to top that by completing it with an even "tinier" final clause; students will stretch their minds to find tinier and tinier clauses. Then have students form five-person teams, each receiving an index card with a different beginning for a hyperbole. Beginnings to print on the cards include:

I am so cold that . . . , I am so tall that . . . , The sea was so rough that . . . , That road was so slippery that . . . , I am so brilliant that . . . , and He was so set that. . . .

Each group completes the hyperbole by writing on the card and then passing it on to other groups, until at least four groups have added a hyperbole to the card. The last group reads the sequences of four hyperboles.

F. Analyzing Lesson Sequences

Students who have participated in poetry workshops consisting of experiences such as those described above should return to identify instructional strategies they themselves can use as part of similar poetry workshops they structure with elementary schoolchildren. Students can also generalize from their workshop experiences and formulate a series of "shoulds" and "should nots" about how to trigger expression.

G. Creating Creative Thinking and Writing Sequences

Provide pre- and in-service teachers with duplicated lines from an Edward Lear alphabet sequence such as:

The Melodious Meritorious Mouse, who played a Merry Minuet
    on the Piano-forte.

The Nutritious Newt, who purchased a Round Plum-pudding for
    his Granddaughter.

The Obsequious Ornamental Ostrich, who wore Boots to keep
    his Feet quite dry.

The Perpendicular Purple Polly, who read the Newspaper and ate
    Parsnip Pie with his Spectacles.

Show the pictures that accompany these lines in Lear's <u>Complete Nonsense Book</u> (Dodd, 1912),and read some of the other outrageous lines. Have teachers, in groups, follow the listening time with group work in which they create an instructional sequence for use with sixth-graders that takes off from the Lear line. Several groups can share their plans with the class by actually involving fellow teachers in the lesson they have planned.

WRITING AS IDEA MAKING

H. Creating with Films

Two short films--<u>The Story of a Book</u>, which describes Holling C. Holling's approach to writing, and <u>Let's Write a Story</u>, which presents visual story starters for elementary students--can be the basis for a session during which teachers develop a learning sequence to use with elementary students. Again, this can be a group planning-together time, with the created plans being shared later with the class.

I. Analyzing Theory and Research Relationships

Here are questions to use in reference to the Forum on page 253 and 266.

1. What is the nature of creative thinking? How can we engage children in creative thinking?

2. What are the advantages and disadvantages of journals?

J. Reporting on Individual and Group Activities

You will find a list of books that relate to children's writing and school writing programs at the end of Chapter Eight in the text itself. In addition, here is a list of articles that students can read and share through oral reports and panel discussions.

Barone, Dian, and Jonathan Lovell. "Bryan and Brave: A Second Grader's Growth as Reader and Writer. <u>Language Arts</u>, 64(September 1987): 505-515.

Blackburn, Ellen. "Common Ground: Developing Relationships Between Reading and Writing." <u>Language Arts</u>, 61(April 1984): 367-375.

Coughlan, Michael. "Let the Students Show Us What They Know." <u>Language Arts</u>, 65(April 1988): 375-378.

D'Alessandro, Marilyn. "The Ones Who Always Get the Blame: Emotionally Handicapped Children Writing." <u>Language Arts</u>, 64(September 1987): 516-522.

Dudley-Marling, Curtis. "Microcomputers, Reading, and Writing: Alternatives to Drill and Practice." <u>The Reading Teacher</u>, 38(January 1985): 388-391.

Dyson, Anne. "Research Currents: Young Children as Composers." <u>Language Arts</u>, 60(October 1983): 884-891.

_____. "Who Controls Classroom Writing Contexts?" <u>Language Arts</u>, 61(October   1984): 618-626.

_____. "Research Currents: The Space/Time Travels of Story Writers." <u>Language Arts</u>, 66(March 1989): 330-340.

Friedman, Sheila. "If You Don't Know How to Write, You Try: Techniques That Work in First Grade." <u>Language Arts</u>, 38(February 1985): 516-521.

Gambrell, Linda. "Dialogue Journals: Reading-Writing Interaction," The Reading Teacher, 38(February 1985): 512-515.

Graves, Donald, and Jane Hansen. "The Author's Chair." Language Arts, 60(February 1983): 176-183.

Hall, Nigel, and Rose Duffy. "Every Child Has a Story to Tell." Language Arts, 64(September 1987): 523-529.

Hansen, Jane. "Authors Respond to Authors." Language Arts, 60(November/December 1983): 970-976.

Hart, Bill. "When the Principal Asks: 'Why Are Your Kids Writing during Reading?'" The Reading Teacher, 41(October 1987): 88-90.

Hess, Mary Lou. "All About Hawks or Oliver's Disaster: From Fact to Narrative." Language Arts, 66(March 1989): 304-308.

Jackson, Louise, et al. "Dear Teacher, Johnny Copied." The Reading Teacher, 41(October 1987): 22-25.

Johnston, Patricia, A Scenic View of Reading." Language Arts, 66(February 1989): 160-170.

Lee, Joyce. "Topic Selection in Writing: A Precarious but Practical Balancing Act." The Reading Teacher, 41 (November 1987): 180-184.

Manning, Maryann, et al. "Journals in First Grade: What Children Write." The Reading Teacher, 41(December 1987): 311-315.

Mikkelsen, Nina. "The Power of Story." Language Arts, 64(January 1987): 61-72.

Spaulding, Cheryl. "Understanding Ownership and the Unmotivated Writer." Language Arts, 66(April 1989): 414-422.

Staton, Jana. "ERIC/RCS Report." Language Arts, 65(February 1988): 198-201.

Taberski, Sharon. "From Fake to Fiction: Young Children Learn about Writing Fiction." Language Arts, 64(October 1987): 586-596.

Tchudi, Susan. "Writer to Reader to Self: The Personal Uses of Writing." Language Arts, 64(September 1987): 489-496.

Tway, Eileen. "Six Bland Method and the Writing Elephant." Language Arts, 60(March 1983): 343-345.

Voss, Margaret. "Make Way for Applesauce: The Literate World of a Three Year Old." Language Arts, 65(March 1988): 272-278.

Zancanella, Don. "On the Nature of Fiction Writing." Language Arts, 65(March 1988): 238-244.

IV. EXAMINATION QUESTIONS

A. Short Discussion Questions

1. What is idea clustering? How would you use it as part of your writing program?

2. For each item on the chart, first create an example of that language usage. Then briefly describe an activity to help children handle each of these elements of written style as part of a study of poetry.

Simile		Metaphor	
Alliteration		Onomatopoeia	

3. Compose a cinquain or a haiku.

4. A principal asks you, "What do you feel is most important in teaching children to write?" How would you answer him or her?

5. Describe four kinds of prose writing forms you believe should be part of elementary writing programs.

6. A child writes a letter:

Dear Grandma,

    Thank you for your birthday present.
It was nice.

    Love,

    Joey

Describe how you would help Joey write more creatively.

7. Describe three ways to encourage kindergartners and first-graders to write.

B. Multiple-Choice Questions

1. In speaking of the creative process, Jerome Bruner would <u>not</u> say
   a. Creating is a paradoxical process.
   b. Creating is the act of a whole person.
   c. The product makes the creative process good and worthy.
   d. A creative act produces effective surprise.
   e. Creating requires both detachment and commitment.

2. According to Bruner, a creative piece comes off lickety-split, finished in the first draft in a form that the writer likes,
   a. Always.
   b. Usually.
   c. Occasionally.
   d. Never.

3. As Bruner uses the term <u>deferral</u> in reference to the creative act, he means the need to
   a. Defer the teaching of writing until children know the alphabet.
   b. Defer drafting until one has thoroughly studied the topic.
   c. Stand back after a period of time and look, with a fresh eye, at what one has drafted.
   d. Defer any kind of writing until one has talked out ideas in the mind or with others.

4. As Bruner uses the term <u>domination</u> in reference to the creative act, he means the
   a. Power of a piece-in-process to compel the writer to complete it.
   b. Control a writer has over his or her creative powers.
   c. Control a writer has to organize his or her ideas into a logical framework.
   d. Domination of the teacher over the creative process in school writing programs.

5. Creativity can be manifested in the writing of
   a. Stories.
   b. Poems and stories.
   c. Poems, stories, and letters.
   d. Poems, stories, letters, and accounts.
   e. Poems, stories, letters, accounts, and reports.

6. Which of the following is <u>not</u> true about beginning writing?
   a. Children should be encouraged to talk about their writing.
   b. Drawing is a part of early writing.
   c. For young children, reading and writing are parts of one whole.
   d. Children must spell correctly before they can write creatively.
   e. Both c and d.

7. Of the following, which does your book <u>not</u> advocate as part of writing for children in grades K-1?
   a. Stress on correct spelling.
   b. Individual dictation.
   c. Slotting.
   d. Group dictation.

8. Research shows that three- and four-year-olds demonstrate
   a. No understanding of the nature of written messages and no understanding of written forms of their language.
   b. No understanding of the nature of written messages but some understanding of written forms of their language.
   c. No understanding of written forms of their language but some understanding of the nature of written messages.
   d. Impressive understanding of written forms of their language and the nature of written messages.

9. Children in the preletter stage of writing may understand that print
   a. Tells a story.
   b. Goes from left to right.
   c. Goes from top to bottom.
   d. All of the above.

10. Children in the random letter stage of writing have *not* learned that
    a. There is a relationship between sounds and letters.
    b. Symbols on paper tell a story.
    c. Written messages are written in lines.
    d. Writing has a purpose.

11. Today educators view invented spelling as
    a. Scribble that should be encouraged.
    b. Scribble that should not be encouraged.
    c. A form of beginning writing that should be encouraged.
    d. A form of beginning writing that should be discouraged.

12. In classroom writing, emphasis should be on
    a. Spelling and usage.
    b. Ideas.
    c. Form.
    d. Correctness.

13. In what kind of story do magical things happen and magical beings exist?
    a. A fantasy.
    b. A mystery.
    c. A fable.
    d. A tall tale.
    e. A work of historical fiction.

14. What would be a satisfactory ending for a haiku that begins "The delicate bough/Bends with its burden of snow"/
    a. And snaps in the wind.
    b. Awaiting the rising moon's glow.
    c. Swings in the freshening breeze--then snaps.
    d. Newly fallen snow/The delicate bough.

15. Which of the following is exemplified by "Playing in the snow:/I gather lots of water/To fill up my boots"?
    a. Haiku.
    b. Cinquain.
    c. Senryu.
    d. Tanka.
    e. Free verse.

16. Concrete, or figure, poems are a particularly good medium for introducing students to
    a. Creative use of the sounds of poetry.
    b. Creative ways of designing words on paper.
    c. Creative use of numbers in poetry.
    d. Mind-stretching images.
    e. Clear, forceful words.

17. A child wrote: "One day dull parrot was flying around thinking of how to make friends with the other parrots. They would not let him play games." This child is developing a concept of
    a. Metaphor.
    b. Personification.
    c. Simile.
    d. Analogy.
    e. Onomatopoeia.

18. Lear's lines "The Absolutely abstemious Ass, who resides in a barrel, and only lived on Soda Water and Pickled Cucumbers" can be used to introduce young people to
    a. Rhythm and rhyme.
    b. Alliteration.
    c. Simile.
    d. Metaphor.
    e. Acronyms.

19. "The man's nose looked like a big red pin cushion" is an example of
    a. Personification.
    b. Alliteration.
    c. Metaphor.
    d. Simile.
    e. Acronym.

20. Of the following, which describe(s) young children as language users?
    a. They have little curiosity about their world.
    b. Their language is expanding slowly.
    c. They are egocentric creatures.
    d. They are independent as writers.
    e. All of the above.

CHAPTER 9

THE WRITING PROCESS--FUNCTIONING AS AN AUTHOR

I. CHAPTER THEMES--WHAT IS INTENDED

Chapter 9 describes steps in the writing process (rehearsal, drafting,
revision, and sharing) and explains the relationship between reading and
writing. It also gives ideas for actively involving children in all aspects of
the writing process and provides check lists for assessing children's growth as
young authors.

II. CHAPTER GOALS--WHAT IS TO BE LEARNED

Having read the chapter, one should be able to state:

    I can state the rationale for teaching writing as process.

    I can explain ways to involve students in (a) reading as a foundation for
writing, (b) rehearsing prior to and during writing, (c) drafting with the
mindset that what is put down is only a beginning, (d) revising what they have
drafted, and (e) sharing what they have written.

    I can use check lists and evaluate criteria to assess children's growth as
writers.

III. IDEAS FOR CREATIVE ENCOUNTERS WITH LANGUAGE AND WITH INSTRUCTIONAL
      STRATEGIES

A. Survey of Chapter 9

Ask students to think about the title of the chapter, brainstorm ideas relative
to the title, and record those ideas above the title web on the first page of
the chapter. Encourage students to survey the chapter headings and the summary
paragraph at the end of the chapter and to write questions or predictions to
guide their reading. Have them note these items beneath the title web from
lines attached to it. Remind students that in college texts there is often
space around the title where they can record "Getting Ready to Read" notes.
Tell them that they can use a similar "Getting Ready to Read" strategy with
children as they prepare to read a selection from a content-area textbook,
except children record on paper rather than in their texts. Use Chapter 9,
Master 1 to guide the prereading study when done as a class activity.

B. On a Yellow Ball Afternoon

Sometime during a course in language arts, you may wish to involve pre- and in-service teachers in a Yellow Ball Afternoon so that they can both get the feel for oral experiences in which children are immersed in language sounds, structures, and meanings and also rehearse for writing. Activities to include in the session may be a combination of the following:

1. A cooperative composing and editing experience. A story-building tower works nicely with college-level students who are learning about teaching. Simply distribute five story puzzle pieces (<u>monster</u>, <u>hole</u>, <u>centipede</u>, <u>slipped</u>, and <u>hollered</u>) to five participants, asking them to mount the pieces in place on the board--or display story-building words using Chapter 9, Master 2. Guide the group in orally composing a story (using the words shown from top to bottom of their story-building tower in sequence) as a scribe records on the board. Then guide participants in cooperatively editing the story by combining sentences, deleting words, expanding sentences, checking punctuation, substituting more exciting words for less interesting ones, and titling the piece. When participants are satisfied with their production, they can read it, expressing punctuation with sounds and gestures. Stop to analyze the word <u>centipede</u> and to identify other words that are built out of <u>centi</u>- or -<u>pede</u>.

     At some point, encourage pre- and in-service teachers to return to identify the kinds of statements and questions you used to guide both creation and editing. It is helpful in this instance to tape the session and have teachers listen to the tape later to analyze your strategies.

2. Direct a choral reading or speaking that stresses interpretation of meanings expressed through punctuation and word repetitions. One piece that is particularly sound-filled is the following:

     We are all <u>nodding</u>, <u>nid</u>, <u>nid</u>, <u>nodding</u>.
     We are all <u>nodding</u>
     At our house at home.
     With a turning in and a turning out,
     And it's this way, that way, round about,
     We are all <u>nodding</u>, <u>nid</u>, <u>nid</u>, <u>nodding</u>,
     We are all nodding
     At our house at home.

Write out just the one verse on charting paper to display during the speaking. Ask participants to invent additional stanzas: "What other things could we be doing at our house?" In the original verse, other stanzas go on to say: We are all sewing, sew, sew, sewing; We are all reading, read, read, reading; We are all spinning, spin, spin, spinning. Each suggestion can be chorused in turn. Incidentally, you can change the periods first to exclamation marks and then to question marks as participants rechorus suggestions and change their intonation patterns to reflect the punctuation marks.

3. Work with some confusing aspect of work usage--such as <u>there</u>, <u>their</u>, and <u>they're</u>, which even college students slip up on periodically. Display sentence strips, perhaps on the central area of the classroom floor, around the perimeter of which participants should sit during the Yellow Ball Afternoon:
     There is my pencil.   I went there.
     Their book is ripped.   I went to their room.
     They're the winners.   Today they're arriving by plane.

Participants group their sentences into three piles, according to the meaning of <u>there</u>, <u>they're</u>, and <u>their</u>, and generalize about the meaning communicated by each. As follow-up, everyone makes three cards, one with each word, and takes turns saying a sentence with one of the three words. Listeners should respond by holding up the appropriate card. If time permits, have each participant writes a sentence (on the reverse side of each card) showing the appropriate usage and meaning of that word.

4. <u>A report</u>. A class member can report on one of the suggested topics included in any of the chapters of this guide.

C. Participating in Learning About Writing

1. You may wish to demonstrate how oral composition can be used to teach a particular skill, such as the use of transitional words to carry story action forward. To do this, share a familiar story; a fairy tale works well. In the sharing, include many transitional words and phrases. Whenever you hit one of those words or phrases, hang a colored piece of oaktag on which the word or phrase has been printed on a story clothesline. After completing the story, take down the tags and distribute them among participants. State that participants are now going to compose a story together using these same words and phrases to keep the story going. If you started with <u>Once</u> and have that written on an oaktag piece, story composing will get off to an easy start. Other words and phrases you may wish to include are:

<u>Suddenly</u>, <u>Now</u>, <u>One day</u>, <u>Then</u>, <u>On the next day</u>, <u>After that</u>, <u>When</u>, <u>And so</u>, <u>Quickly</u>, <u>But</u>, <u>To make matters worse</u>, <u>Every morning</u>, <u>Every evening</u>, and <u>However</u>.

2. Conduct a brainstorming of facts and a classification of those facts similar to the procedure followed by Ms. Amos. Topics about which teachers will have a storehouse of available facts to contribute include automobiles, cats, energy, Switzerland, and Japan.

3. Read aloud a story such as <u>Patrick</u>, Arlene Mosel's <u>The Funny Little Woman</u> (Dutton, 1972), or <u>The Magic Tree</u>. College-level listeners can concoct storymaps based on the tale. Later, in groups, students can create original maps that tell a story. A group representative can then share the story with other groups, using the map as a display outline.

4. An alternative activity is to read aloud a story such as Algernon Black's <u>The Woman of the Wood</u> (Holt, Rinehart & Winston, 1973) or Eric Carle's <u>The Mixed-up Chameleon</u> (Crowell, 1975). College-level listeners can concoct story staircases or flow charts based on the tale heard and go on to create original story staircases or flow charts for stories of their own invention. This latter creation can be individual, with students eventually joining in small story-sharing groups and telling their stories in turn to others in the group.

D. Analyzing Teaching

Use these questions to help teachers-to-be understand the purposes and strategies demonstrated in the Teaching-in-Action vignette in the chapter. Structure the questions as a class or small-group discussion. In the latter case, reproduce the questions in the form of a discussion guide.

THE WRITING PROCESS

1. What specific writing skills was Mr. Kamolsky interested in children acquiring and mastering? Are these skills significant? Why? Why not?

2. How did he use the following teaching strategies to achieve his goals?

    a. Factstorming.
    b. Categorizing and charting.
    c. Teacher-guided group writing.
    d. Teacher-guided group editing.
    e. Team writing and editing.

3. What difficulties do you see in his approach? How could you restructure the lesson to overcome these difficulties?

4. What advantages do you see in his approach?

5. What do you think is meant by <u>learning through writing</u>? How does that expression differ from <u>learning to write</u>?

6. Think of another context--rather than a social studies unit review--in which you could use a comparable sequence of activities: factstorming, categorizing/charting, teacher-guided group writing, teacher-guided group editing, and team writing and editing.

7. Compare and contrast Mr. Kamolsky's lesson sequence with Ms. Amos's on pages 306-308 of the text. How are they similar? How are they different?

8. Donald Graves talks of the need for rehearsal before writing. How did both Kamolsky and Amos allow for rehearsal before writing?

Also use Chapter 9, Master 3 to talk about the instructional strategies Mr. Kamolsky used.

E. Analysis of Theory

Discuss the questions at the end of the Forum in Chapter 9. Then use chapter 9, Master 4 to summarize with the class key aspects of the writing process. Suggest that students keep their books open and refer to related pages as they present points. Ask for volunteers to add points directly to the projected transparency. Remind students that they can use summary transparencies in a similar way as they teach language arts and reading skills as part of content-area studies. In conclusion, remind students of Dan Kirby's warning about marching students through the writing process in lock-step fashion as set forth in the Forum.

F. Reporting on Individual and Group Activities

Here are readings that can serve as the basis for individual and/or group reports. The first group of readings is restricted to items that explain the early work of Donald Graves and his associates. The second group is more general.

Barrs, Myra. "The New Orthodoxy about Writing: Confusing Process and Pedagogy." Language Arts, 60(October 1983): 829-840. Presents a critique of the research done by the New Hampshire group.

Calkins, Lucy. "Andrea Learns to Make Writing Hard." Language Arts, 56(May 1979): 569-576.

_____. "Children Learn the Writer's Craft." Language Arts, 57(February 1980):207-213.

_____. Lessons from a Child. Portsmouth, N.H.: Heinemann Educational Books, 1983.

_____. "When Children Want to Punctuate: Basic Skills Belong in Context." Language Arts, 57(May 1980): 567-573.

Graves, Donald. "Examination of the Writing Processes of Seven-Year-Old Children." Research in the Teaching of English, 9(Winter 1975): 227-241.

_____. "How Do Writers Develop?" Language Arts, 59(February 1982): 173-179.

_____. "Let's Get Rid of the Welfare Mess in the Teaching of Writing." Language Arts, 53(September 1976): 645-651.

_____. A Researcher Learns to Write: Selected Articles and Monographs. Portsmouth, N.H.: Heinemann Educational Books, 1984.

_____. "Research Update: Where Have All the Teachers Gone?" Language Arts, 58(April 1981): 492-497.

_____. "Teacher Intervention in Children's Writing." Language Arts, 60(October 1983): 841-846.

_____. "What Children Show Us about Revision." Language Arts, 56(March 1978): 312-319.

_____. Writing: Teachers and Children at Work. Portsmouth, N.H.: Heinemann Educational Books, 1983.

Graves, Donald, and Susan Sowers. "A Six-Year-Old's Writing Process: The First Half of First Grade." Language Arts, 56(October 1979): 829-835.

Kamler, Barbara. "One Child, One Teacher, One Classroom: The Story of One Piece of Writing." Language Arts, 57(September 1980): 680-693.

Turbill, Jan, ed. No Better Way to Teach. Portsmouth, N.H.: Heinemann Educational Books, 1983.

Walshe, R. D., ed. Donald Graves in Australia: "Children Want to Write. . . ". Portsmouth, N.H.: Heimemann Education Books, 1981. A compilation of articles, some of which appear in this bibliography.

Other references:

Austin, Patricia. "Brian's Story: Implications for Learning through Dialogue."
    Language Arts, 66(February 1989): 184-192.

Bissex, Glenda. "Growing Writers in Classrooms." Language Arts, 58 (October
    1981): 785-791.

Carroll, Joyce. "Project ALERT--Process Writing." Language Arts, 58 (March
    1981): 301-307.

Clay, Marie. "Learning and Teaching Writing: A Developmental Perspective."
    Language Arts, 59(January 1982): 65-70.

Cowin, Gina. "Implementing the Writing Process with Sixth Graders: Jumaji,
    Literature Unit." The Reading Teacher, 40(November 1986): 156-161.

Crane, Irene. "Holistic Scoring--A Technique That Encourages Creativity in
    Writing." The Reading Teacher, 40(December 1986): 369-370.

Fine, Esther. "Marbles Lost, Marbles Found: Collaborative Production of Text."
    Language Arts, 64(September 1987): 474-487.

Fitzgerald, Jill. "Helping Young Writers to Revise: A Brief Review for
    Teachers." The Reading Teacher, 42(November 1988): 124-129.

Guilbault, Janie. "Between the Lines: An Affective Look at Real-Life Writing."
    Language Arts, 65(September 1988): 461-464.

Haley-James, Shirley. "Helping Students Learn Through Writing." Language
    Arts, 59(October 1982): 726-731.

Hennings, Dorothy. "A Writing Approach to Reading Comprehension." Language
    Arts, 59(January 1982): 8-17.

Holbrook, Hilary. "Writing to Learn in the Social Studies." The Reading
    Teacher 41(November 1987): 216-219.

Jacobs, Suzanne. "Investigative Writing: Practice and Principles." Language
    Arts, 61(April 1984): 356-363.

Jett-Simpson, Mary. "Writing Stories Using Model Structures: The Circle
    Story." Language Arts, 58(March 1981): 293-300.

Kostelny, Susan. "Development of Beginning Writing Skills Through a Total
    School Program." The Reading Teacher, 41(November 1987): 1156-1159.

Mayher, John, and Nancy Lester. "Putting Learning First in Writing to Learn."
    Language Arts, 60(September 1983): 717-722.

Oboyski-Butler, Kathy. "Sharing the Job of Evaluation." Language Arts,
    66(April 1989): 407-422.

Russell, Connie. "Putting Research into Practice: Conferencing with Young
    Writers." Language Arts, 60(March 1983): 333-345.

Ruth, Leo. "Reading Children's Writing." The Reading Teacher, 40(April 1987): 756-760.

Samway, Katharine. "Formal Evaluation of Children's Writing: An Incomplete Story." Language Arts, 64(March 1987): 289-298.

Smith, Frank. "Myths of Writing." Language Arts, 58(October 1981): 792-798.

Willinsky, John. "The Writer in the Teacher." Language Arts, 61(October 1984): 585-591.

Winkeljohann, Sister Rosemary. "How Do We Help Children with the Conventions of Writing?" Language Arts, 58(October 1981): 862-863.

Zaharias, Jane. "Microcomputers in the Language Arts Classroom." Language Arts, 60(November/December 1983): 990-997.

IV. EXAMINATION QUESTIONS

A. Short Discussion Questions

1. Explain why reading is important for young authors. Then describe two ways to encourage children to read.

2. Describe three specific ways to involve children in rehearsing before drafting.

3. Explain how factstorming and webbing can be used to help children see relationships among ideas. Through your answer demonstrate that you know the meaning of factstorming and webbing.

4. Describe approaches to drafting you could use to help children as they draft ideas on paper.

5. To help a student develop self-critical powers in a personalized conference, the teacher guides the student by asking questions. Provide three questions--each emphasizing a different aspect of writing--that you could ask a part of a conference to get a child to think through his or her writing.

6. Describe two strategies for involving young authors in revising. Do not describe the personalized conference.

7. Explain why sharing is important in involving children in the writing process. Describe two ways to encourage the sharing of writing.

B. Multiple-Choice Questions

1. Comparing young people's writing skills in 1975 with those in 1969, NAEP found
    a. A substantial increase in student' abilities to write in 1975.
    b. A minor increase in students' abilities to write in 1975.
    c. No change in students' writing skills.
    d. An erosion of skills from the 1969 levels.

2. In the 1980s, NAEP reported that young people lack the ability to
   a. Analyze and evaluate what they read.
   b. Analyze what they read, but they can evaluate it.
   c. Evaluate what they read, but they can analyze it.

3. To teach children to write, teachers must involve them in
   a. The writing process.
   b. Grammar study.
   c. Writing followed by teacher correction of errors.
   d. Writing followed by teacher correction of errors and the preparation of a final, corrected draft.
   e. All of the above.

4. Which statement best sums up the relationship between good writers and reading?
   a. Good writers do more voluntary reading than poor ones do.
   b. Good writers do very little reading.
   c. Good writers generally do not like to read.
   d. There is a negative relationship between good writing and increases in reading experiences.

5. Reading aloud to students is a valuable activity for
   a. Lower-primary children.
   b. Middle-graders.
   c. Upper-elementary children.
   d. All of the above.

6. Which of the following can be part of writing?
   a. Pictorializing.
   b. Talking to oneself before and during writing.
   c. Talking informally to peers.
   d. Talking informally to the teacher prior to and during writing.
   e. All of the above.

7. Rehearsing is important in the writing of
   a. Stories.
   b. Informational pieces.
   c. a. and b.

8. Of the following, which is the most logical sequence to teach children to see relationships among ideas?
   a. Factstorming, webbing, and fact gathering.
   b. Fact gathering, factstorming, and webbing.
   c. Fact gathering, webbing, and factstorming.
   d. Webbing, fact gathering, and factstorming.
   e. Webbing, factstorming, and fact gathering.

9. In drafting, children should be taught to
   a. Be neat the first time through.
   b. Use copy-editing symbols, cross out, and insert.
   c. Use their very best handwriting.
   d. All of the above.

10. The researcher who has given us many ideas about revision and the writing conference is
    a. Graves.
    b. Haynes.
    c. Bissex.
    d. Veal.

11. Children draft more compositions than they revise. They should revise those compositions which
    a. Have the most errors.
    b. Have the least errors.
    c. Are chosen for publication.
    d. Are the most creative.
    e. Are the least creative.

12. Reading aloud during revision and editing is helpful in identifying
    a. Punctuation problems.
    b. Sentence beginnings.
    c. Misspellings.
    d. Awkwardness in expression.
    e. All of the above.

13. The teacher's job during a writing conference is to
    a. Elicit information.
    b. Show the student where he or she has done well.
    c. Show the student where he or she has gone wrong.
    d. Correct the student's mistakes and tell the student about them.
    e. All of the above.

14. According to Cramer, the basis of an editing workshop is
    a. A child's first draft.
    b. A child's final draft.
    c. Material from the basal reading text.
    d. Material from content-area texts.
    e. All of the above.

CHAPTER 10

LANGUAGE PATTERNS, USAGE, AND GRAMMAR--
MANAGING IDEAS

I. CHAPTER THEMES--WHAT IS INTENDED

Chapter 10 presents a rationale and activities for learning to control the
sentence and for learning about oral- and written-language usage patterns and
grammar. It may be read in conjunction with Chapters 2 and 9.

II. CHAPTER GOALS--WHAT IS TO BE LEARNED

Having read the chapter, one should be able to state:

    I can describe a series of activities for developing sentence sense that
include sentence expansion, transformation, combining, inserting, and
reconstruction.

    I can design sessions in which students discover language generalizations
and apply them in writing.

    I can list patterns for structured writing and, in literature sources, can
locate other such patterns to use.

    I can select stories to involve children in the conventions of written
usage.

    I can describe ways to teach sentencing, paragraphing, capitalization,
punctuation, and usage so that students use these things in their writing.

    I can explain the purpose of grammar study and outline ways to make
grammar come alive.

    I can create more activities that help students appreciate their language.

III. IDEAS FOR CREATIVE ENCOUNTERS WITH LANGUAGE AND WITH
      INSTRUCTIONAL STRATEGIES

A. Survey of Chapter 10

Ask students to think about the title of the chapter, brainstorm ideas relative
to the title, and record those ideas above the title web on the first page of

the chapter. Encourage students to survey the chapter headings and the summary paragraph at the end of the chapter and to write questions or predictions to guide their reading. Have them write these items beneath the title web from lines attached to it. Remind students that in college texts there is often space around the title where they can record "Getting Ready to Read" notes. Tell them that they can use a similar "Getting Ready to Read" strategy with children as they prepare to read a selection from a content-area textbook, except that children record their webs on paper rather than into a text. Use Chapter 10, Master 1 to guide the prereading study when done as a class activity.

B. Analyzing the Teaching-in-Action Vignette

Analyze the Teaching-in-Action vignette that opens the chapter (Jeanne Smith and "The Rooster and the Pearl.") Use Chapter 10, Master 2 as the basis for interaction. Provide students with duplicate copies of the master to complete as volunteers add points to the projected transparency.

C. Working with Story Reconstruction

A portion of a college class session in language arts methodology can profitably be spent listening to a story, reconstructing it from story cards, introducing appropriate punctuation, and generalizing about punctuation usage from specific instances, much in the same manner as the opening exercise of Chapter 10. Of course, pre- and in-service teachers will go on to identify teaching strategies, assumptions, and goals, as well as limitations of the techniques. For this you will need a story to read, story summary cards, and punctuation markers, including quotation marks. For your convenience, here are summary phrases to use with McDermott's The Magic Tree (Holt, Rinehart & Winston, 1973):

Luemba and Mavungu
were brothers
The ugly, unloved brother Mavungu
decided to leave home
Mavungu
found a beautiful princess
The princess said
I want to be his wife but he is ugly

The princess also said
I want to be his wife
    but he is raggedy
She
made him strong and
    handsome
and pledged him to silence
Mavungu
promised never to reveal
the source of wealth and
    pleasure

Having read the laboratory story orally, distribute the cards at random, and encourage participants in session to order the cards and add punctuation marks, in each case explaining why. Then have participants, in groups, produce several more story strips with punctuation to finish the story. Story cards can be laid out on the floor so all can see. (You may want to ask a member of the class to prepare and lead this session, basing his or her lesson on the one supplied at the beginning of Chapter 10.)
    Incidentally, The Magic Tree is a fine story for a discussion of right and wrong. This instructor has used it by asking such questions as:

How many of you think that Mavungu was wrong to do what he did? Very wrong--shake your fist. A little wrong--hold up your hand. O.K.--make an O. Very right--clap.
Why do you think Mavungu did what he did? What motivated him? Describe when you have been motivated by the same feelings.
Was his punishment too severe? too lenient? just? Why?
Was Mavungu's mother more wrong than Mavungu?
Was Mavungu's wife wrong to pledge Mavungu to silence? Why did she do this?   Rank-order the three characters in terms of extent of wrongness-- Mavungu's mother, Mavungu, and Mavungu's wife.

Having involved teachers in making value judgments, this instructor then asks them to identify the kinds of questions used to trigger judgmental thinking.

C. Analysis of Episodes

Ask students in work teams to do the following:

1. Identify the assumptions underlying the episode that opens Chapter 10 and the one experienced directly with The Magic Tree. How are the assumptions similar? How are they different?

2. Identify specific techniques shared by the two lessons.

3. Discuss the limitations of using the floor as a composing stage, and list alternative ways to achieve the same effect.

D. Creating Story Reconstruction Cards

Distribute basal readers intended for students in grades 3 and 4 to groups of pre- and in-service teachers. Groups working together must do the following:

1. Select a story from the basal reader.

2. Construct story reconstruction cards for it. Groups should consider what specific written-language usage skills can be developed through story reconstruction and the resetting of punctuation marks.

3. Prepare to guide a group in reconstructing the story and resetting the punctuation.

Later, groups can be reshuffled so that memberships change.

E. Analyzing Language Arts Textbook Series

Bring to class several language arts textbooks with differing emphases. Ask students in grade-level groups to analyze books for that grade level from several series. Students should do the following:

1. Identify the proportion of the text allocated to grammar study.

2. Identify the proportion of the text allocated to communication processes.

3. Judge the creativity of the exercises and the interest level of the content and illustrations.

4. Identify specific ways that newer concepts of grammar developed by the historical, structural, and transformational grammarians have been incorporated.

5. Summarize the kinds of learnings stressed in each textbook.

The above points, as well as those listed under C and D above, can be duplicated and distributed in the form of a Team Task Card.

F. Analyzing Theory

Use these questions in reference to the Forums on pages 359 and 370.

1. What is Roy Clark's point of view on teaching writing skills?

2. What is Lucy Calkin's point of view on the teaching of writing skills, especially punctuation skills? Do you agree or disagree? Why?

3. What would be necessary in a writing program that adheres to the philosophy of skills teaching espoused by Calkins and Clark?

4. What is Patrick Groff's rationale for the teaching of grammar? Given that reasoning, what proportion of language arts in elementary schools should be dedicated to the teaching of grammar? Should other language learnings take precedence over the learning of grammar? Explain your reasoning.

G. Sharing Creative Grammar Ideas

Each pre- or in-service teacher can devise one innovative activity for developing with children an understanding and an appreciation of their language. Ask each teacher to bring to class all required materials, as well as a handout describing the activity. Then have each speak for a few minutes, explaining the how and why behind the activity devised; participants should leave the session with a booklet-like packet of creative teaching ideas. The session can be billed as a Cooperative Workshop.

H. Reviewing Knowledge of Grammar and Parts of Speech

Display a card that reads <u>The fly fell into the lemon pie</u>. Ask students to tell you what part of speech the word <u>fly</u> is. When they say <u>noun</u>, ask them to prove to you that the word is a noun. Proofs students give should include the following:

1. <u>Fly</u> is the name of a thing. Nouns are names of persons, places, and things. (Tell students that this is a traditional definition--that linguists have developed other ways of viewing a noun.)

2. <u>Fly</u> functions as the subject of the sentence. Nouns function, or work, as subjects, as objects of verbs, and as objects of prepositions. (Ask students

to contrast this proof with that in item 1: whereas item 2 focuses on the way a word functions in a sentence, item 1 focuses on the word divorced from a sentence context. Tell students that modern-day linguists prefer to view parts of speech in terms of the context in which a word operates--the sentence.)

3. Fly patterns with the word The, which is a noun marker, or determiner. Nouns tend to pattern with determiners. (Tell students that, again, they are looking at a linguistic approach to parts of speech.)

4. Fly can be made plural to signify more than one. Fly can be made possessive. Nouns are words that can be used in plural and possessive forms. (Suggest that this is another linguistic, rather than traditional grammar approach to defining a noun. In this case, the proof is in terms of inflectional endings that typify nouns.)

5. Tell students to look in their texts to identify one other characteristic of noun words. Have them identify suffixes that characterize noun words and give examples of words in sentences that bear these suffixes and function as nouns.

Having considered nouns in this fashion, run through a similar series of proofs for verbs. Encourage students to keep their books open to the section of Chapter 10 titled "The Four Major Classes of Words" and to scan it for points during the discussion.

To help organize the discussion, display Chapter 10, Master 3 and provide students with a copy for recording their own discussion notes. Ask volunteers to record points on the projected transparency during the discussion.

I. Reporting on Individual and Group Activity

Readings that provide content for individual and group reports include the following:

Calkins, Lucy. "When Children Want to Punctuate." In Donald Graves in Australia. ed. R. Walshe, Exeter, N.H.: Heinemann Educational Books, 1981.

Cordeiro, Patricia, et al. "Apostrophes, Quotation Marks, and Periods: Learning Punctuation in the First Grade." Language Arts, 60(March 1983): 323-332.

Cudd, Evelyn. "Transformations." The Reading Teacher, 42(December 1988): 263-264.

ERIC/RCS Report. "Orthodoxies in Language Instruction." Language Arts, 64(April 1987): 416-420.

Gallagher, Nora. How to Stop a Sentence and Other Methods of Managing Words. Reading, Mass.: Addison-Wesley, 1982.

Greenhalgh, Carol, and Donna Townsend. "Evaluating Students' Writing Holistically--An Alternative Approach." Language Arts, 58(October 1981): 811-822.

LANGUAGE PATTERNS, USAGE, AND GRAMMAR

Hubbard, Ruth.   "Second Graders Answer the Question, Why Publish?"   The Reading Teacher, 38(March 1985): 658-663.

Susi, Geraldine.   "Christian and the Question Mark: A Story of Ownership."   The Reading Teacher, 40(November 1986): 132-134.

Weaver, Constance.   Grammar for Teachers: Perspective and Definitions.   Urbana, Ill.: National Council of Teachers of English, 1979.

IV.   EXAMINATION QUESTIONS

A.   Short Discussion Questions

1.   The suggestion is given that you parallel the teaching of a punctuation convention with writing that calls for a pattern to be learned. Show how that works by citing several punctuation conventions and related writing assignments.

2.   Describe two specific techniques you can use in introducing young children to the way sentences begin and end.

3.   Describe three activities through which children in grade 3 or above can learn about the way nouns (or adjectives, if you prefer) operate in sentences.

4.   Compose a diamante. Then explain the contribution it can make to children's understanding of their language.

B.   Multiple-Choice Questions

1.   In what form should a teacher record children's written expression for them?
   a.   In paragraph fashion.
   b.   Without capitalization.
   c.   Without punctuation.
   d.   With each sentence on a separate line.
   e.   With each sentence as a new paragraph.

2.   In teaching children to handle noun-verb agreement, the teacher should begin
   a.   With oral language generated by students.
   b.   By stating the rules that should be applied.
   c.   By helping children select the correct words to be used in exercise sentences.
   d.   With written samples of the language as used.

3. The generalizing stage of language study takes place
   a. During the introductory phase of a language-learning sequence.
   b. After children have generated numerous sentences with the same usage pattern.
   c. Before children generate numerous sentences with the same usage pattern.
   d. Never in elementary classrooms; this stage belongs in secondary schools.

4. How would most language arts experts evaluate the assignment "Learn the seven usages of the comma"?
   a. As very valuable.
   b. As only moderately valuable.
   c. As a waste of time.

5. Linguists of today believe that a grammar describes
   a. How the language originated.
   b. How the language changed.
   c. How words pattern in sentences and phrases.
   d. Correct language usage.
   e. All of the above.

6. Latin is a poor model on which to base English grammar because
   a. Latin depends more on function words to communicate meanings than English does.
   b. English depends more on word order to communicate meanings than Latin does.
   c. English depends more on inflectional endings to communicate meanings than Latin does.

7. Syntactic clues are used today as a base for differentiating parts of speech. Syntactic clues include
   a. Affixes and inflections associated with a particular part of speech.
   b. Function words that pattern with a particular part of speech.
   c. Characteristic positions in a sentence occupied by a part of speech.
   d. All of the above.
   e. None of the above.

8. Children in school learn about nouns, verbs, and so forth primarily to
   a. Increase their ability to read and write.
   b. Increase their ability to speak and listen.
   c. Increase their ability to use their language in creative ways.
   d. Help them understand and appreciate the way their language communicates meanings.

9. Techniques recommended in your text for learning grammar include
   a. Underlining and/or circling particular parts of speech.
   b. Analyzing samples of language generated by learners.
   c. Learning lists of words that can function as a particular part of speech.
   d. Placing parts-of-speech abbreviations above words in sentences.
   e. All of the above.

10. Modern linguists would be <u>least</u> happy with definitions of nouns as
    a. Names of people, places, and things.
    b. Words that have a plural form.
    c. Words that have a possessive form.
    d. Words that can have their place taken by pronouns.
    e. Words that can be signaled by determiners.

11. Students turning statements into questions are involved with
    a. Subordination.
    b. Transformation.
    c. Combining, or coordination.
    d. Negation.
    e. Expansion.

12. A major way to help students overcome the run-on problem is to work with sentence
    a. Patterns.
    b. Transformations.
    c. Combining.
    d. Expansion.
    e. Negation.

13. Skill in composing sentences most probably comes from
    a. Memorizing the definition of a sentence.
    b. Filling in the blanks of many sentences.
    c. Copying sentences corrected by the teacher in compositions.
    d. Writing and manipulating sentences.
    e. All of the above.

CHAPTER 11

SPELLING, DICTIONARY USE, AND HANDWRITING--
TOOLS OF THE EDITOR'S CRAFT

I. CHAPTER THEMES--WHAT IS INTENDED

Chapter 11 describes the stages in children's spelling development and offers
suggestions for a spelling program in which understanding of word patterns and
relationships is more important than memorization of individual words. Chapter
11 also identifies learnings about dictionary use and describes ways to
introduce children to manuscript and forms of cursive handwriting.

II. CHAPTER GOALS--WHAT IS TO BE LEARNED

Having read the chapter and completed the skill-building activities at the end
of each section, one should be able to state the following:

    I can describe the stages in children's spelling development.

    I can structure spelling lessons so that children inductively discover
the sound-symbol relationships, within-word patterns, and word-building
patterns in English and can apply their understanding as they encounter new
words in the content areas.

    I can supplement linguistic approaches with activities and games that
involve children visually and kinesthetically.

    I can structure a spelling program that relies on both grouping and
individual study agenda to meet individual differences and needs.

    I can identify spelling errors children tend to make and can identify
spots in words where such errors are likely to occur.

    I can explain skills and appreciations fundamental to using a dictionary
as a writing tool and ways to achieve these learnings with children.

    I can structure a handwriting sequence that introduces children
systematically to manuscript or cursive forms and provides meaningful practice
in real writing situations.

    I can help children diagnose their own handwriting problems and design
handwriting experiences through which individual correct those problems.

III. IDEAS FOR CREATIVE ENCOUNTERS WITH LANGUAGE AND WITH
      INSTRUCTIONAL STRATEGIES

A. Survey of Chapter 11

Ask students to think about the title of the chapter, brainstorm ideas relative
to it, and record those ideas above the title web that opens the chapter.
Encourage students to survey the chapter headings and the summary paragraph at
the end of the chapter and to write questions or predictions to guide their
reading. Have them write these items beneath the title web from lines attached
to it. Remind students that in college texts there is often space around the
title where they can record "Getting Ready to Read" notes in similar fashion.
Tell them that they can use a similar "Getting Ready to Read" strategy as
children prepare to read a selection from a content-area textbook. Children,
of course, record their prereading thoughts on paper, not in their books. Use
Chapter 11, Master 2 to guide the prereading study when done as a class
activity.

B. Use Chapter 11, Master 2 as the basis of a discussion of stages in
children's spelling development. Students who have read the text·and studied
the Henderson chart in it provide details to complete the master. Refer
students to the part openers of Communication in Action for examples of
children's spelling that fit into the Henderson categories.

C. Looking at Error Patterns

College students can identify typical error patterns by analyzing their own
invented spellings. Begin by dictating a list of spelling demons--words such
as desert, buoy, proceed, vacuum, complementary, nucleus, souvenir, all right,
pressure, and rhinoceros. Have students correct their own papers and identify
places where they made letter deletions, additions, transpositions, or
substitutions, and where they confused one word with another. In each case,
have them hypothesize reasons for the way they spell a word and consider how
knowledge about error patterns should affect their way of teaching spelling.

D. Structuring Spelling Lessons

Pages from any commercial spelling text can serve as content for a class
session in which pre- and in-service teachers in teams design an inductive
lesson sequence for use with a spelling group. Participants should do the
following:

1. Produce an overall plan for a lesson sequence in which children discover
the intended generalization and apply their discovery in work with other words
and in editing their writing.

2. Prepare materials such as word cards or blocks to use in teaching the
lesson.

3. Create follow-up, gamelike activities.

4. Develop a possible individualized study agenda for students in the group.

Items 1-4 above can be duplicated and distributed as a Team Task sheet.

E. Comparing Spelling Series

If your institution owns several spelling series, use them as the basis for a comparative session. Give teams, organized according to grade levels, several different texts for use at the designated level and compare the following items.

1. The kinds of broad spelling learnings being taught.

2. The specific words chosen for inclusion and grouped together in weekly lists.

3. The possibility of using the material in inductive sessions.

4. The creativity and interest value of the follow-up activities.

5. The stresses and ideas given in the teacher's guide.

6. The attempts to integrate other language arts and curricular areas.

7. The overall design of the book--index, glossary, format, and so forth.

Again, these points can be duplicated and supplied to analytical teams.

F. Introducing a Thesaurus

Use pages from W. Cabell Greet's thesaurus In Other Words (Scott, Foresman, 1968) as content for another "planning-for-teaching" session. Teams of pre- or in-service teachers should:

1. Study the pages to discover the overall design of the material on a particular theme.

2. Plan a creative sequence through which a group of middle-graders would actually use that material.

3. Print the steps in the sequence on a chart to share with others during a follow-up session.

G. Improving Your Writing

Zaner-Bloser will supply college instructors of the language arts with complimentary manuscript, transition cursive, and adult cursive work sheets that are particularly helpful with preservice teachers who need attention to their own handwriting. Distributed at the end of a class session and taken home, these work sheets review letter formation and provide guided practice for needy undergraduates.

H.   Spelling-Handwriting Materials

As an out-of-class assignment, preservice teachers can produce a set of materials to use in teaching handwriting or spelling, or can create a game. These materials can be shared with classmates during a Materials-Sharing Workshop.

I.   Analyzing Teaching

Use chapter 11, Masters 3 and 4 in reference to the Teaching-in-Action vignettes on pages 385-388, 412-416, 422-425. In addition, use these questions.

1.   What goals did Mr. Bronsky have in mind as he taught the spelling lesson? What did he do to achieve his objectives? What is an inductive teaching sequence? In what respect was this an inductive teaching sequence?

2.   Compare and contrast Ms. Robinson's lesson on manuscript writing with Mr. Bronsky's lesson on cursive writing. Based on the two lessons, generalize about what is important in handwriting lessons.

J.   Analyzing Theory

Use these questions in reference to the Forums on pages 396, 420, and 430-433.

1.   Why is it important for teachers to function as researchers in their own classrooms? How do you see yourself functioning as a teacher-researcher?

2.   What is Kristine Anderson's view of the "teaching" of spelling? Do you agree or disagree? Why?

3.   What is J. Richard Gentry's view of invented spelling? Do you agree or disagree? Why?

4.   James and Carol Beers talk about children's development of spelling knowledge and skill. What do they say about this important topic? How does their research relate to Henderson's work cited in the running text? What are the implications of all this work for elementary spelling programs?

5.   Do you equate messiness in writing with lack of knowledge? Why or why not? How can you help children see the importance of good handwriting and at the same time indicate to them that ideas are key in writing? In what context does Graves see handwriting being taught? Do you agree or disagree? Why?

K.   Reporting on Individual and Group Activity

Readings that can provide content for individual and group reports include the following:

Anderson, Kristine.   "The Development of Spelling Ability and Linguistic
     Strategies."   The Reading Teacher, 39(November 1985): 140-147.

Beers, James, and Carol Beers. "Vowel Spelling Strategies among First and Second Graders: A Growing Awareness of Written Words." <u>Language Arts</u>, 57(February 1980): 166-171.

Beers, James, and Edmund Henderon. "A Study of Developing Orthographic Concepts among First Graders." <u>Research in the Teaching of English</u>, 2(1977): 133-148.

Betza, Ruth. "Online: Computerized Spelling Checkers: Friends and Foes?" <u>Language Arts</u>, 64(April 1987): 438-443.

DiStefano, Philip, and Patricia Hagerty. "Teaching Spelling at the Elementary Level: A Realistic Perspective." <u>The Reading Teacher</u>, 38(January 1985): 337-377.

Gable, Robert, Jo Hendrickson, and Jane Meeks. "Assessing Spelling Errors of Special Needs Students." <u>The Reading Teacher</u>, 42(November 1988): 112-117.

Ganschow, Leonore. "Analyze Error Patterns to Remediate Severe Spelling Difficulties." <u>The Reading Teacher</u> 38, (December 1984): 288-293.

Gentry, J. Richard, and Edmund Henderson. "Three Steps to Teaching Beginning Readers to Spell." In <u>Developmental and Cognitive Aspects of Learning to Spell</u>, ed. Edmund Henderson and James Beers, 112-119. Newark, Del.: International Reading Association, 1980.

Gillet, Jean, and M. Jane Kita. "Words, Kids, and Categories." In <u>Developmental and Cognitive Aspects of Learning to Spell</u>, ed. Edmund Henderson and James Beers, 120-126. Newark, Del.: International Reading Association, 1980.

Graham, Steve, and Lamoin Miller. "Spelling Research and Practice: A Unified Approach." <u>Focus on Exceptional Children</u>, (October 1979): 1-16.

Harp, Bill. "Why Are Your Kids Giving Each Other Spelling Tests?" <u>The Reading Teacher</u>, 41(March 198): 702-704.

Henderson, Edmund. <u>Learning to Read and Spell</u>. DeKalb, Ill.: Northern Illinois University Press, 1981.

_____. <u>Teaching Spelling</u>. Second edition. Boston: Houghton Mifflin, 1990.

Hodges, Richard. <u>Learning to Spell</u>. Urbana, Ill.: National Council of Teachers of English, 1981.

_____. "On the Development of Spelling Ability." <u>Language Arts</u>, 59(March 1982): 284-290.

Koenke, Karl. "Handwriting Instruction: What Do We Know?" <u>The Reading Teacher</u>, 40(November 1986): 214-216.

Lehr, Fran. "Spelling Instruction: Phonics, Rules, and Word Lists." <u>The Reading Teacher</u>, 38(November 1984): 218-220.

SPELLING, DICTIONARY USE, AND HANDWRITING

Morris, Darrell. "Concept of Word and Phoneme Awareness in the Beginning
     Reader." Research in the Teaching of English, 17(December 1983): 359-
     373.

Nolen, Patricia. "Sound Reasoning in Spelling." The Reading Teacher,
     33(February 1980): 538-543.

Radebaugh, Muriel. "Children's Perceptions of Their Spelling Strategies." The
     Reading Teacher, 38(February 1985): 532-537.

Ramsey, John. "Why Is Left Handed Writing Still a Problem in the Last 7th of
     the 20th Century?" The Reading Teacher, 41(February 1988): 504-506.

Read, Charles. Children's Categorization of Speech Sounds in English. Urbana,
     Ill.: National Council of Teachers of English, 1975.

Richgels, Donald. "Experimental Reading with Invented Spelling (ERIS): A
     Preschool and Kindergarten Method." The Reading Teacher, 40(February
     1987): 522-529.

Rule, Rebecca. "The Spelling Process: A Look at Strategies." Language Arts,
     59(April 1982): 379-384.

Templeton, Shane. "The Circle Game of English Spelling: A Reappraisal for
     Teachers." Language Arts, 56(October 1979): 789-797.

Wasylyk, Thomas. "Teaching Left Handers the Write Stuff." The Reading
     Teacher, 42(February 1989): 446-447.

IV. EXAMINATION QUESTIONS

A. Short Discussion Questions

1. Two kinds of dictionary-related learnings are (a) skills related to
    locating and interpreting entries and (b) appreciation of the dictionary
    as a reference and writing tool. Elaborate on what is meant by each of
    these learnings. For each, detail a specific activity that would
    contribute to children's acquisition of it.

2. Your text states that "meaningful handwriting practice should be provided
    as part of ongoing classroom activity." Describe at least four kinds of
    meaningful work in which handwriting can be a part.

3. Outline a chart that children in early second grade can use to diagnose
    their handwriting weaknesses.

4. Before introducing children to cursive, teachers should take some specific
    instructional first steps. List three preliminaries that can ease
    children's transition from manuscript to cursive.

5. Spelling skill is essentially a tool to be applied as one encounters new
    words. Describe specific ways you can help children apply growing
    spelling skill as they encounter a word such as nucleus in biology study.

6. Describe step by step how you can cycle a weekly spelling program in which you have <u>four</u> different spelling groups.

7. According to your text, in spelling programs based on linguistic concepts learners discover relationships for themselves. In order to make discovery possible, how must you structure spelling sessions?

8. Describe the stages in children's spelling development according to the research evidence available. Include reference to Henderson's findings.

B. Multiple-Choice Questions

1. Linguists such as Hanna, Hodges, and Hanna stress the
   a. Mispronunciations that result in misspellings.
   b. Irregularities in English spelling.
   c. Spelling demons that pose a problem to poor spellers.
   d. Physical feel of writing a word.
   e. Consistencies in the way speech sounds are represented on paper.

2. /d/ written on paper designates a
   a. Morpheme.
   b. Phoneme.
   c. Grapheme.
   d. Word.
   e. Meaning.

3. In spelling programs based on linguistic principles, we would be most likely to find emphasis on
   a. Letter patterns that recur in English spelling.
   b. The shape of the word.
   c. Repetitive practice through writing and rewriting.
   d. Giving children spelling generalizations to learn.
   e. Memorizing rules of spelling that apply with some degree of consistency.

4. A <u>snurk</u> is defined as
   a. A word derived from another language.
   b. A word that has not changed in spelling for more than two hundred years.
   c. A word that does not abide by spelling generalizations.
   d. An antonym.
   e. A synonym that is confounding.

5. Of the following, which one is required as a base for all the others?
   a. A concept of what a word is.
   b. The ability to work with within-word patterns.
   c. The ability to use letter names in spelling.
   d. The ability to manipulate word-building qualities of English.
   e. An understanding of word origins.

6. Teaching by the discovery method, the spelling teacher begins by
   a. Skating the rule to be applied.
   b. Asking questions that help children see how their language operates.
   c. Giving the limitations.
   d. Presenting exceptions to the rule.
   e. Presenting a series of words that adhere to the rule.

7. Which of the following best describes current thinking on the teaching of spelling?
   a. Work with spelling relationships should be part of study in all curricular areas.
   b. Emphasis in upper-grade programs should be on monosyllabic words.
   c. Spelling lists should be composed of words related to a topic, such as Thanksgiving words like turkey, pumpkin, and Pilgrim.
   d. Learning to spell should be a one-step process--a matter of writing the words.

8. Spelling apropos as apropo is an example of
   a. Letter deletion.
   b. Letter addition.
   c. Letter transposition.
   d. Letter substitution.
   e. Confusion of homonyms.

9. In teaching spelling, you should teach
   a. The class as a whole, with all children studying the same lesson during a weekly cycle.
   b. The class in spelling groups, with students mapping out their work on a study agenda.
   c. The children individually by assigning different pages in the text to different children.
   d. The children individually by preparing a separate lesson for each youngster.

10. Visual and kinesthetic clues are particularly helpful as children learn to
    a. Handle sound-symbol relationships.
    b. Handle word-building units of the language.
    c. Interpret dictionary entries.
    d. Spell demons.
    e. Trace etymological clues.

11. The use of a dictionary to find the correct spelling of words becomes feasible when
    a. Children know the most common graphemes used to represent a phoneme.
    b. Children pair off as spelling mates who search together.
    c. The teacher serves as a senior editor who provides searching assistance for difficult words.
    d. The teacher actually supplies the words needed by very young writers.
    e. All of the above.

12. The thesaurus is a reference book that should be found in every classroom, starting in
    a. Lower-elementary grades.
    b. Middle-elementary grades.
    c. Upper-elementary grades.
    d. Junior high school.
    e. Senior high school.

13. Most prehandwriting activity should be carried out as activity
    a. Separated from other curricular study so as to emphasize motor coordination.
    b. Integrated primarily with prereading activity.
    c. Integrated primarily with prespelling activity.
    d. Integrated with both prereading and prespelling activity.

14. In structuring early handwriting sessions, teachers have generally found that it is wisest to
    a. Introduce together letters that are structurally dissimilar.
    b. Emphasize separate letters, with less attention given to writing letters in words.
    c. Provide models of letter forms.

15. The form of cursive used initially by children in the third grade differs from adult cursive in
    a. Letter formation.
    b. Letter formation and slant.
    c. Size and proportion.
    d. Size, proportion, and letter formation.
    e. Size, proportion, letter formation, and slant.

16. The ultimate criterion to apply in judging handwriting is,
    a. Is it legible?
    b. Is it neat?
    c. Are letters written as taught?
    d. Is slant maintained?
    e. Are letters appropriately sized?

17. As children begin to draft ideas on paper, they should
    a. Stop to check spelling.
    b. Stop to check the appropriateness of word meaning with the aid of a dictionary.
    c. Write carefully in their best handwriting.
    d. Do all of the above.
    e. Do none of the above.

CHAPTER 12

READING FOR MEANING--
LEARNING TO READ AND READING TO LEARN

I.   CHAPTER THEMES--WHAT IS INTENDED

Chapter 12 opens with a discussion of ways to help young children begin to read and then presents current ideas about the importance of prior knowledge in comprehension. Included here is a discussion of prereading activity and how to structure it. The chapter continues by outlining levels of reading comprehension and ways of involving readers in the structure of materials they read--story, poem, and informational selections. A final section of the chapter explains ways of encouraging library use.

II.   CHAPTER GOALS--WHAT IS TO BE LEARNED

Having read the chapter and completed the skill-building activities at the end of each section, one should be able to state the following.

     I can explain numerous strategies for teaching young children to read: the shared literary experience, the big-book approach, predictable stories, masking words with tape, matching words, reconstruction of stories, joining-in-while-listening, reading and writing captioned books, reading-along-while-listening, choral reading, paired reading, imitative oral reading, and one-to-one reading. I can design lessons that include one or more of these strategies.

     I can explain the significance of schemata in reading and reading instruction. I can explain ways of organizing reading instruction to help children draw on their prior knowledge as they generate meaning in reference to a text.

     I can list steps to take in prereading a text.

     I can distinguish among literal, interpretative, critical, and creative reading; and I can devise questions in reference to a text at each of these levels.

     I can describe ways to actively involve children in the structure of stories and poems, particularly ways to involve children with metaphorical use in literature.

     I can explain how to actively involve children in the structure of informational passages. I can give the rationale for relating reading and writing activity. I can give a rationale for relating reading and talking in elementary classrooms.

I can describe ways to involve children in library use.

I can explain the use of miscue analysis and informal reading inventories in assessing children's early reading development.

III. IDEAS FOR CREATIVE ENCOUNTERS WITH LANGUAGE AND WITH
      INSTRUCTIONAL STRATEGIES

A. Survey of Chapter 12

Ask students to think about the title of the chapter, brainstorm ideas relative to it, and record those ideas above the title web that opens the chapter. Encourage students to survey the chapter headings and the summary paragraph at the end of the chapter and to write predictions or questions to guide their reading. Have them write these items beneath the title web from lines attached to it. Remind students that in college texts they often find space around the title where they can record "Getting Ready to Read" notes. Tell them that they can use a similar "Getting Ready to Read" strategy as children prepare to read a selection from a content-area textbook. Children, of course, record their prereading thoughts on paper, not in their books. Use chapter 12, Master 2 to guide the prereading study when done as a class activity.

B. Analysis of the Teaching-in-Action Vignette: "The Communication Circle"

Use Chapter 12, Master 2 as (a) a transparency to guide students' analysis of the Teaching-in-Action vignette that opens the chapter or (b) a small-group Task Sheet. Also use these questions:

1. How did Ms. Wilkening make words an integral part of her classroom?

2. How did Ms. Wilkening prepare her children for reading and give them some prior experiences related to what they would read?

3. What levels of questions did Ms. Wilkening project in relation to the story? In what ways did she develop her question to help children comprehend the structure of the story?

4. Ms. Wilkening taught skills as an integral part of her lesson. How did she develop children's auditory discrimination skills? ability to progress from left to right? sight-word vocabulary? spelling skills? visual discrimination skills? sequencing skills?

5. How did Ms. Wilkening integrate reading, writing, and talking in her classroom? Do you think this is easy to do? Why or why not?

6. Would you like to teach the way Ms. Wilkening does? Why or why not?

C.   Thinking about Reading Theory

1.   After students have read the sections in their text on emergent reading, lead a general discussion or workshop session in which they describe specific ideas for involving children in reading. Use Chapter 12, Master 3 as the basis for the session, with students adding points to the master projected with an overhead projector.

2.   Project Chapter 12, Masters 4 and 5, or distribute them as handouts. Ask students in groups to complete the guides through discussion based on their reading of the text. Follow up with total-class interaction in which students add points to the projected masters.

3.   Demonstrate to the class the way to share a big book. Sources of big books include Scholastic Press (New York, NY) and Rigby Education (454 South Virginia Street, Crystal Lake, IL 60014). This instructor particularly likes The Three Billy Goats Gruff from Rigby. Share the book by introducing the cover and encouraging students to (a) predict based on the cover and (b) join in on the repeating phrases. Share the book again, again encouraging students to join in on parts they remember. Then demonstrate how a teacher can highlight the decoding of a particular grapheme--in this case gr, as in grass, Gruff, and great. Ask students how the words are similar at the beginning; ask for other words that begin with the same sound. Then reread the story, with listeners joining in on all the words that begin with gr.

After students have enjoyed a big-book experience, discuss these questions:

o   What are the purposes of a big-book experience?

o   How does the teacher organize the experience?

o   What kinds of activities can be part of a big-book experience?

o   What is the philosophy behind a big-book experience?

o   How is the big-book experience similar to and different from a language experience activity (LEA)?

4.   Here are questions to use with the Forum on page 453.
      a.   What is Meeks's view of reading?
      b.   How does Meeks's description of reading compare with what you do when you read?
      c.   How can you teach children to do the kinds of things Meeks describes as they read?

5.   Here are questions to use with the Forum on page 443.

a.   What has Alison learned about the nature of print? How has she learned this? What implications for the teaching of beginning reading can we draw from the discussion of Harste, Woodward, and Burke?

b.   What is Denny Taylor telling us about the way young children learn about the world of print? How is Taylor's work similar to that of Harste, et al.?

6. Here are questions to use with the Forum on page 456.

a. According to Wittrock, what is involved in full comprehension? What does this imply about the kinds of reading materials students should encounter in school reading programs?

b. Does James Squire appear to agree with Wittrock on the nature of children's reading experiences?

D. Being Part of a Learning Environment

Demonstrate a way of triggering children's prior knowledge relative to a text to be read by involving pre- or in-service teachers in a brainstorming/conceptual webbing/reading/talking sequence. A good story text to use for this purpose is Lucille Clifton's My Friend Jacob. As an introduction to the story, ask participants what a friend is, what their friends and friendships mean to them, what they do with their friends, how to make friends, and what words are synonyms for friendship. Record words and ideas brainstormed higgledy-piggledy over the board. In brainstorming, contribute key story words that deal with friendship and that participants overlook. Get children talking, using these words; this is a way to ensure that children have an understanding of words before encountering them in reading. When the board is filled, go back and organize the items according to relationships offered by participants. In other words, have them put together all synonyms for friendship, all items that tell things friends do together, and so forth. When participants have sorted the items to their liking, ask them to read the story to find out what else is involved in friendship and how the friendship in the story is particularly special. Then have participants add thoughts to their web of friendship.

    Instead of using My Friend Jacob and the idea of friendship as the content for brainstorming/webbing/reading/talking, you may want to use a nonfiction selection intended for adult reading to demonstrate this approach to prior knowledge. This instructor has successfully used columns from the op-ed page of a big-city newspaper as the focus for such a session.

E. Preparing for Teaching

1. Pre- and in-service teachers of reading should have some opportunity to design experiences and questions to use in guiding children's reading. To this end, distribute storybooks to groups of teachers or teacher-to-be and ask them to:

a. Plan a prereading talk-time based on the book received. Based on the content of the story and its structure, participants should put together a sequence of things to do that helps trigger children's prior experiences.

b. Plan a series of questions to use following the reading of the story that taps children's comprehension of it--comprehension that reflects attention to story structure and at the same time goes beyond a literal grasp of the story.

c. Lay out the sequence and questions on charting paper for future sharing with the total class.

After three-person teams have completed this assignment, ask them to share their output with the rest of the class. Listeners should listen to see whether they can add related ideas.

2. Participants can prepare and bring to class a teaching material they could use to teach beginning reading. Such a material could be an original big book with masks to cover words or word cards for matching, a story cut up for reconstruction, a poetry chart for choral reading, materials to go along with a predictable story, or materials to trigger creation of a captioned book by children. Schedule an Idea Fair in which participants share their productions.

3. Participants can study several related sections of a basal reading text and decide how they could use this material in a creative way. Good for this purpose is the final unit, "Summershine," of the Riverside Readings Program's fourth-grade reader Grand Tour (Riverside Publishing, Chicago, 1989). Share poems from the unit, including James Tippett's "Sunning," Nikki Giovanni's "Knoxville, Tennesse," and Carl Sandburg's "Summer Grass"; also share the story "McBroom's Ear" by Sid Fleischman and the informational selection "Sunflowers." Organize participants in small groups, and ask them to propose an integrated language arts "game plan" for teaching these selections as children anticipate their summer vacations. A game plan should include:

a. Proposed activities.

b. A list of reading skills to be stressed.

c. A list of listening/speaking/writing skills to be acquired through study.

d. Related readings for independent follow-up.

4. Divide the class into small groups to analyze and evaluate basal reading series used in classrooms. Studying each book in a series, along with the teacher's edition, participants should ask the following questions and give examples of each instance:

a. Are there selections by respected children's writers?

b. Is there a good cross section of story, poem, and informational matter?

c. Does the art complement the verbal aspects?

d. Are the passages teachable in that the creative teacher can devise worthwhile and exciting ways to use them?

e. Does the teacher's edition provide ideas for writing, listening, and speaking?

f. Does the teacher's edition provide activities for teaching basic comprehension skills? Can these activities be modified to meet individual needs?

Use Chapter 12, Master 6 to prepare a handout for the group task talk.
F. Locating Teaching Materials

Pre- and in-service teachers can locate stories and poems that they believe are particularly good for developing children's understanding of story/poem structures and plot motifs. In a seminar Sharing Workshop, have participants explain why their selections are particularly applicable.

G. Creating Original Stories and Poems

As teachers consider aspects of literary comprehension, they themselves will gain an understanding of what is involved by actually listening, identifying a pattern, and then trying it out firsthand. A good introduction is "This Is the House That Jack Built."

This is the <u>house</u> that Jack built.
This is the <u>malt</u>, that lay in the house that Jack built.
This is the <u>rat</u>, that ate the malt, that lay in the house that Jack built.
This is the <u>cat</u>, that killed the rat, that ate the malt, that lay in the house
    that Jack built.
This is the <u>dog</u>, that worried the cat, that killed the rat, that ate the malt,
    that lay in the house that Jack built.
This is the <u>cow</u> with the crumpled horn, that tossed the dog, that worried the
    cat, that killed the rat, that ate the malt, that lay in the house that
    Jack built.
This is the <u>maiden</u> all forlorn, that milked the cow with the crumpled horn,
    that tossed the dog, that worried the cat, that killed the rat, that ate
    the malt, that lay in the house that Jack built.
This is the <u>man</u> all tattered and torn, that kissed the maiden all forlorn, that
    milked the cow with the crumpled horn, that tossed the dog, that worried
    the cat, that killed the rat, that ate the malt, that lay in the house
    that Jack built.
This is the <u>priest</u> all shaven and shorn, that married the man all tattered and
    torn, that kissed the maiden all forlorn, . . .
This is the <u>cock</u> that crowed in the morn and waked the priest all shaven and
    shorn, that married the man all tattered and torn, that . . .

Share it several times, with teachers joining in on successive repetitions. Then begin an original class version that builds sequentially the way the original does. A possible beginning for class composing is "This is a picture that Paul painted . . ." Or allow time for group or individual composing. Here is a version--created by Patti Silia, a sixth-grader in Woodbridge, New Jersey--that you may want to share with teachers after they have created versions of their own:

             "This is the Flea that Fell on my Knee"

This is the <u>flea</u> that fell on my knee.
This is the <u>mouse</u>, that went after the flea that fell on
    my knee.
This is the <u>bird</u>, that ate the mouse, that went after
    The flea that fell on my knee.
This is the <u>bee</u>, that stung the bird, that ate the mouse,
    that went after the flea that fell on my knee

This is the <u>cat</u>, that went after the bee, that stung the
    bird, that ate the mouse, that went after the flea
    that fell on my knee.
This is the <u>dog</u>, that chased the cat, that went after the
    bee, that stung the bird, that ate the mouse, that went
    after the flea that fell on my knee.
This is the <u>tick</u>, that bit the dog, that chased the cat,
    that went after the be, that stung the bird, that ate
    the mouse, that went after the flea that fell on my knee.
This is the <u>flea</u>, that found the tick, that bit the dog,
    that chased the cat, that went after the bee, that
    stung the bird, that ate the mouse, that went after the
    flea that fell on my knee.

THE END

H. Summarizing Key Ideas

Use Chapter 12, Masters 7 and 8 to summarize key approaches to reading.

I. Reporting on Individual and Group Activities

Students can read and report on these articles:

Combs, Martha. "Modeling the Reading Process with Enlarged Texts." <u>The
    Reading Teacher</u>, 40(January 1987): 422-426.

Cunningham, Patricia, and James Cunningham. "Content Area Reading-Writing
    Lessons." <u>The Reading Teacher</u>, 40(February 1987): 506-513.

Flood, James. "The Text, The Student, and the Teacher: Learning from
    Exploitationn in Middle Schools." <u>The Reading Teacher</u>, 39(April
1986): 784-791.

Flynn, Linda. "Teaching Critical Reading Skills through Cooperative Problem
    Solving." <u>The Reading Teacher</u>, 42(May 1989): 664-669.

Harden, Krista. "Reading to Remember." <u>The Reading Teacher</u>, 40(February
    1987): 580-582.

Harp, Bill. "Why Are You Doing Guided Imagery during Reading Time?" <u>The
    Reading Teacher</u>, 41(February 1988): 588-590.

Heald-Taylor, Gail. "How to Use Predictable Books for K-2 Language Arts
    Instruction." <u>The Reading Teacher</u>, 40(March 1987): 656-663.

Holmes, Betty, and Nancy Roser. "Five Ways to Assess Readers' Prior
    Knowledge." <u>The Reading Teacher</u>, 40(March 1987): 646-649.

McCallum, Richard. "Don't Throw the Basals Out with the Bath Water." <u>The
    Reading Teacher</u>, 42(December 1988): 204-208.

Nessel, Denise. "The New Face of Comprehension Instruction: A Closer Look at Questions [DRTA]." The Reading Teacher, 40(March 1987): 604-606.

Palincsar, Annemarie, and Ann Brown. "Interactive Teaching to Promote Independent Learning from Text." The Reading Teacher, 39(April 1986): 771-777.

Piccolo, Jo Anne. "Expository Text Structure." The Reading Teacher, 40(May 1987): 838-847.

Strickland, Dorothy et al. "Research Currents: Classroom Dialogue during Literature Response Groups." Language Arts, 66(February 1989): 192-200.

Templeton, Shane. "Literacy, Readiness, and the Basal." The Reading Teacher, 39(January 1986): 403-409.

Valencia, Sheila, and P. David Pearson. "Reading Assessment: Time for a Change." The Reading Teacher, 40(April 1987): 726-732.

Weiss, Maria. "A Key to Literacy: Kindergartners' Awareness of the Functions of Print." The Reading Teacher, 41(February 1988): 574-578.

Wong, Jo Ann, and Kathryn Hu-pei Au. "The Concept-Text-Application Approach: Helping Elementary Students Comprehend Expository Text." The Reading Teacher, 38(March 1985): 612-618.

Wood, Karen. "Guiding Students through Informational Text." The Reading Teacher, 41(May 1988): 912-920.

IV. EXAMINATION QUESTIONS

A. Short Discussion Questions

1. Open-book question: Compare Ms. Wilkening's session with any other episode that opens or is contained within a chapter of your textbook. Select for this purpose an episode that you believe is most similar to Ms. Wilkening's, and describe the points of similarity. Indicate the assumptions under which you believe both teachers are operating and the goals each is trying to achieve.

2. Open-book question: Contrast Ms. Wilkening's session with any other episode that opens or is contained within a chapter of your textbook. Select for this purpose an episode that you believe is most dissimilar from Ms. Wilkening's, and describe the points of difference. Indicate the assumptions under which both teachers are operating and the goals each is trying to achieve.

3. Describe one activity that you could use as part of a shared literary experience to teach each of the following skills:

a. Left-to-right progression.
b. Visual discrimination.
c. Use of contextual skills.
d. Auditory discrimination.

4. Select any nursery rhyme, fable, or fairy tale with which you are familiar. Use "The Three Bears" if you wish.

a. Either write questions or describe an activity that you could use to develop children's understanding of story structure.

b. Write questions that you could use to get children thinking at the literal, interpretative, critical, and creative levels.

5. Explain the meaning of <u>readability</u>. What problems exist with the use of readability formulas?

B. Multiple-Choice Questions

1. According to an interactive theory of reading, what a reader comprehends depends on
   a. What the reader brings to the text.
   b. What the author has put into the text.
   c. Both a. and b.

2. The major philosophy about skills teaching in reading espoused by <u>Communication in Action</u> is that
   a. Many skills can be taught as part of natural reading activity.
   b. No skills can be taught as part of the ongoing reading act.
   c. Reading skills are discrete entities and thus must be taught individually.
   d. Reading skill must be taught separate from other language and communication skills.
   e. Both c. and d.

3. What is meant by a <u>big book</u> as the phrase is used by Holdaway?
   a. A picture storybook.
   b. A classic such as <u>Alice in Wonderland</u>.
   c. A book that child readers already know.
   d. A book enlarged so that groups of children can see the print.
   e. A book written by a well-known, or "big," author such as Dr. Seuss.

4. The networks of prior information that readers bring to reading are called
   a. Schemata.
   b. Cohesion.
   c. Big books.
   d. Major memory.
   e. Limited-access memory.

5. What is meant by <u>paired reading</u>?
   a. Children's skill in reading is paired with selections they read.
   b. Two children read orally together.
   c. A child confers one-on-one with the teacher.
   d. A child reads orally to the teacher.

6. Cutting up story sentences into meaningful phrases and having children reconstruct the story sentences is a technique to help children recognize that
   a. Language works in chunks of meaning.
   b. Words are composed of individual sounds.
   c. Sentences are composed of separate words.
   d. Stories have a structure.

7. In your text, reading along while listening is presented as a way to teach children to
   a. Practice phonics skills.
   b. Comprehend truly complicated prose selections.
   c. Comprehend story structure.
   d. Group words in chunks of meaning.

8. Oral reading by children is useful to determine
   a. Children's comprehension of a text.
   b. Children's ability to read with flair and feeling.
   c. Children's ability to reflect punctuation signals in reading.
   d. Children's ability to phrase words in chunks of meaning.
   e. All of the above.
   f. b, c, and d.

9. By prior knowledge, as the phrase is applied to reading, we mean what readers
   a. Know and believe about a subject on which they are reading.
   b. Know about the way language works.
   c. Know about how ideas are organized in written form.
   d. Know about the way different literary forms are structured.
   e. All of the above.
   f. a. and b.

10. When we talk about readers' interacting with what they read, we are talking about
    a. Oral reading.
    b. Creating meaning in reading.
    c. Talking to others about reading.
    d. A shared literary experience.
    e. Very fast reading.

11. According to Vygotsky, what happens to egocentric speech as children mature? It
    a. Increases.
    b. Diminishes.
    c. Become internalized.
    d. Both a. and c.
    e. Both b. and c.

12. At what level(s) is prereading classroom talk important?
    a. At the primary level.
    b. At the upper-elementary level.
    c. At the high school level.
    d. All of the above.
    e. a. and b.

13. Brainstorming and conceptual webbing are presented as means of handling
    a. Stories and informational selections.
    b. Vocabulary of selections before reading.
    c. Relationships among words and ideas.
    d. All of the above.
    e. b. and c.

14. A suggestion such as "Let's compose a story that teaches the same lesson" is asking children to function at the
    a. Interpretive level.
    b. Critical level.
    c. Literal level.
    d. Creative level.

15. A question such as "Which act in the story was the most horrible?" is asking children to function at the
    a. Interpretive level.
    b. Critical level.
    c. Literal level.
    d. Creative level.

16. Asking children to tell where a story takes place when that information is stated directly in the story is asking them to function at the
    a. Interpretative level.
    b. Critical level.
    c. Literal level.
    d. Creative level.

17. Asking children to tell why a character acted the way he or she did when this information is not stated directly in the text is asking them to function at the
    a. Interpretative level.
    b. Critical level.
    c. Literal level.
    d. Creative level.

18. In regard to sustained silent reading, your textbook takes
    a. No definitive position.
    b. A positive position.
    c. A negative position.

19. The phrase story structure refers to the
    a. Way a story works.
    b. Details of a story.
    c. Theme of the story.
    d. Main idea.

20. Metacognition refers to a person's
    a. World knowledge.
    b. Linguistic knowledge.
    c. Understanding of how text is structured.
    d. Awareness of how he or she learns, knows, and reads.
    e. Ability to use phonics to decode.

21. SQ3R is an approach most suitably applied to reading of
    a. Informational prose.
    b. Poetry.
    c. Fairy tales.
    d. Novels.
    e. Tall tales.

22. When used as a teaching strategy, modeling helps children comprehend the structure of
    a. Stories.
    b. Poems.
    c. Both a. and b.
    d. Neither a. nor b.

23. About reading for sequence, James Squire believes that
    a. Reading for sequence in a short story is different from reading for historical sequence.
    b. Reading for sequence in a short story is different from reading for sequence in a process article.
    c. Reading for sequence in a short story is different from reading for historical sequence and for sequence in a process article.
    d. Reading for sequence is the same in any context.

24. Which of these is involved in preview skimming of an informational selection?
    a. Answering the questions at the end of the selection.
    b. Writing summaries of each major section.
    c. Reading for the main idea and supporting details.
    d. Reading the title and subheads, and predicting what the selection is about and how it is organized.

25. Which of the following best represents the position put forth by your textbook?
    a. Teaching of reading and writing cannot be divorced from one another.
    b. Teaching of reading and talking cannot be divorced from one another.
    c. Teaching of reading and writing should be divorced from one another.
    d. Teaching of reading and talking should be divorced from one another.
    e. c. and d.
    f. a. and b.

26. Children should be given assistance in using the library starting
    a. Early in kindergarten.
    b. At the end of kindergarten.
    c. In the first grade.
    d. Early in the second grade.
    e. No sooner than the third grade to prevent confusion.

27. The teacher masks a word on a story chart and asks children to figure out what that word might be. The teacher is working on
    a. Use of context clues.
    b. Left-to-right progression.
    c. Sound-symbol relationships.
    d. Story structure.

28. According to Swaby, as part of an analysis of a reader's miscues, the teacher should ask
    a. How well does he or she use phonic information in reading?
    b. How well does he or she use syntactic information in reading?
    c. How well does he or she use semantic information in reading?
    d. How well does he or she monitor reading and correct his or her own miscues?
    e. All of the above.
    f. b., c., and d.

29. Readability formulas are used to
    a. Identify a child's miscues.
    b. Analyze a child's miscues.
    c. Determine the level of difficulty of a text.
    d. Determine whether a child is promoted to the next grade level.

30. What is meant by a think-aloud as part of reading instruction?
    a. Predicting and talking before reading.
    b. Reading aloud and telling the thoughts that come to mind.
    c. Reading aloud.
    d. Talking about a selection before and after reading it.
    e. Reading aloud a paragraph a reader has written about a selection.

31. The primary purpose of an after-reading Literature Group as devised by Watson is to
    a. Test students' ability to comprehend story structure.
    b. Test students' literal comprehension.
    c. Teach children to phrase higher-level questions as they read.
    d. Teach children to socialize and function with one another.
    e. Teach children to use phonics and sight words as decoding tools.

32. What is the key element of Manzo's Guided Reading Procedure?
    a. Making a matrix chart.
    b. Having students ask questions modeled after those the teacher asks.
    c. Talking about personal feelings and reactions after reading.
    d. Brainstorming points after reading and then rereading to add and correct points.
    e. Demonstrating mind talk.

33. What is the key element of Brown's reciprocal teaching activity?
    a. Making a matrix chart.
    b. Having students ask questions modeled after those the teacher asks.
    c. Talking about personal feelings and reactions after reading.
    d. Brainstorming points after reading and then rereading to add and correct points.
    e. Demonstrating mind talk.

CHAPTER 13

CHILDREN WITH LANGUAGE DIFFERENCES AND DIFFICULTIES

I. CHAPTER THEMES--WHAT IS INTENDED

Chapter 13 describes the language learning problems of exceptional children in regular classrooms. It focuses specifically on the language-gifted, the language-slow, the language-different, and those with impairments in hearing, vision, and speech. Suggestions are given on ways to diagnose children's language problems.

II. CHAPTER GOALS--WHAT IS TO BE LEARNED

Having read the chapter, one should be able to state:

    I can describe ways to help children who are becoming bilingual or bidialectal.

    I can explain strategies for working with gifted and slow learners.

    I can describe ways of helping children with impairments in hearing, vision, and speech.

    I can explain the rationale for continuous diagnosis of children's language development and can use check lists to assess children's needs for specific language learning experiences.

III. IDEAS FOR CREATIVE ENCOUNTERS WITH LANGUAGE AND WITH
       INSTRUCTIONAL STRATEGIES

A. Survey of Chapter 13

Ask students to think about the title of the chapter, brainstorm ideas that come to mind relative to the title, and record those ideas on the title web on the first page of the chapter. Encourage students to survey the chapter headings and the summary paragraph at the end of the chapter and to write questions or predictions to guide their reading. Have them write these items beneath the title web from lines attached to it. Remind students that in college texts there is often space around the title where they can record "Getting Ready to Read" notes. Tell them that they can use a similar "Getting Ready to Read" strategy with children preparing to read a selection from a content-area textbook; children create a prereading web on a separate sheet of paper. Use Chapter 13, Master 1 to guide the prereading study when done as a class activity.

B. Analysis of Teaching-in-Action Vignette: A Nature Outing for All

After students have read the chapter, involve them in a class discussion of the opening vignette. Ask them first to describe the activities the teacher used and then to tell why she did as she did. Project Chapter 13, Master 2 during the discussion, and have a student scribe record key points on it as they emerge from the discussion.

C. Building Background Knowledge

Ask students to complete the guide in Chapter 13, Master 3 as they read the chapter. During follow-up discussion, display the guide with an overhead projector. Ask students to provide data to add to the projected transparency.

D. Listening to the Experts

In colleges and universities having a special education division, specialists in the various aspects of instruction for exceptional children can address the language arts class to extend the information given in the text.

E. Sharing Findings

In preparation for a seminar session, have each participant read a journal article of his or her choosing on ways to help dialectally different or language-different children to grow in language facility; ask participants to use a Note Card to the significant points raised in the articles. During a round-table discussion session, you may initiate interaction by asking such questions as the following: Why are there different dialects of a language? How is a dialect different from a language? What is the origin of black English? How does black English differ from standard English? What specific techniques did you encounter for helping children acquire a second dialect? What is the current feeling about dialectal readers? What specific techniques did you encounter for helping children acquire a second language? What is the relationship between language and culture? If participants have read widely, they will be able to bring many diverse opinions to bear on these questions.

F. Analyzing Theory

Use these questions with the Forums on pages 502 and 505 of Chapter 13.

1. What "false notions" about English dialects does Robbins Burling point out? When he identified phonological characteristics of black English dialects, with what is he concerned? With what is he concerned when he identifies syntactic characteristics?

2. How do you view the phonological and syntactic characteristics of black English dialects--as different? as deficient? How will your point of view

influence your teaching?
3. What should be the focus of remedial reading programs according to Allington and the Shumakers?

G. Reporting on Individual and Group Activity

Readings that can serve as content for individual and group reports are as follows:

THE LANGUAGE-DIFFERENT CHILD

Commins, Nancy. "Language and Affect: Bilingual Students at Home and at School." Language Arts, 66(January 1989): 29-43.

Feeley, Joan. "Help for the Reading Teacher with the Limited English Proficient (LEP) Child in the Elementary Classroom." The Reading Teacher, 36(March 1983): 650-655.

Flatley, Joannis, and Adele Rutland. "Using Wordless Picture Books to Teach Linguistically/Culturally Different Students." The Reading Teacher, 40(December 1986): 276-281.

Gillet, Jean, and J. Richard Gentry. "Bridges Between Nonstandard and Standard English with Extensions of Dictated Stories." The Reading Teacher, 36(January 1983): 360-366.

Gonzales, Philip. "How to Begin Instruction for Non-English-Speaking Students." Language Arts, 58(February 1981): 175-180.

Hudelson, Sarah. "The Role of Native Language Literacy in the Education of Language Minority Children." Language Arts, 64(December 1987): 842-854.

Johns, Kenneth. How Children Learn a Second Language. Bloomington, Indiana: Phi Delta Kappa, 1988.

Leibowicz, Joseph. "ERIC/RCS Report: Classrooms, Teachers, and Nonstandard Speakers." Language Arts, 61(January 1984): 88-91.

Moll, Luis. "Some Key Issues in Teaching Latino Students." Language Arts, 65(September 1988): 465-472.

Moustafa, Margaret, and Joyce Penrose. "Comprehensible Input PLUS the Language Experience Approach: Reading Instruction for Limited-English-Speaking Students." The Reading Teacher, 38(March 1985): 640-647.

Neuman, Susan, and Elaine Pitts. "A Review of Current North American Television Programs for Bilingual Children." The Reading Teacher, 37(December 1983): 254-260.

Schon, Isabel, and Patricia Kennedy. "Noteworthy Books in Spanish for Children and Young Adults from Spanish-speaking Countries." The Reading Teacher, 37(November 1983): 138-142.

CHILDREN WITH LANGUAGE DIFFERENCES AND DIFFICULTIES

Sutton, Christine. "Helping the Nonnative Speaker with Reading." The Reading Teacher, 42(May 1989): 684-688.

Tompkins, Gail, and Lea McGee. Launching Nonstandard Speakers into Standard English." Language Arts, 60(April 1983): 463-469.

Walsh, Catherine. "Language, Meaning, and Voice." Language Arts, 64(February 1987): 196-206.

Zupinsky, Bonnie. "Bilingual Reading Instruction in Kindergarten." The Reading Teacher, 37(November 1983): 132-137.

THE EXCEPTIONAL CHILD--GENERAL ARTICLES

Gresham, Frank. "Social Skills Instruction for Exceptional Children." Theory into Practice, 21(Spring 1982): 129-133.

Hutchinson, Thomas, and Norris Haring. "Serving Exceptional Individuals." Theory into Practice, 21(Spring 1982): 82-87.

Raver, Sharon, and Robert Dwyer. "Teaching Handicapped Preschoolers to Sight Read Using Language Training Procedures." The Reading Teacher, 40(December 1986): 314-321.

THE CHILD WITH SPEECH DISORDERS

Perullo, Robert. "Stuttering: You Can Ease the Pain." Instructor, 89(March 1980): 138-139.

Scofield, Sandra. "The Language-delayed Child in the Mainstreamed Primary Classroom." Language Arts, 55(September 1978): 719-723.

THE CHILD WITH HEARING DISORDERS

Carlsen, Maryann. "Between the Deaf Child and Reading: The Language Connection." The Reading Teacher, 38(January 1985): 424-426.

Clark, John, and Elizabeth Pieper. "The Hearing Impaired Child." Instructor, 87(March 1978): 152-154.

Hirsh-Pasek, Kathy. "Beyond the Great Debate: Fingerspelling as an Alternative Route to Word Identification for Deaf or Dyslexic Readers." The Reading Teacher, 40(December 1986): 340-343.

Israelson, Jo. "The Eyes Have It or--Superheroes = Superlanguage." Teaching Exceptional Children, 11(Winter 1979): 57-60.

Manson, Martha. "Explorations in Language Arts for Preschoolers (Who Happen to Be Deaf)." Language Arts, 59(January 1982): 33-39.

Stauffer, Russell. "Language Experience Approach for Deaf and Hearing Impaired Children." The Reading Teacher, 33(October 1979): 21-24.

THE VISUALLY HANDICAPPED

Bader, Lois. "Instructional Adjustments to Vision Problems." The Reading Teacher, 37(March 1984): 566-569.

Cohen, Janet. "Walk a Mile in My Shoes." Instructor, 88(October 1978): 186-187.

McGee, Lea, and Gail Tompkins. "Concepts about Print for the Young Blind Child." Language Arts, 59(January 1982): 40-45.

Rouse, Michael. "Teacher's Guide to Vision Problems." The Reading Teacher, 38(December 1984): 306-317.

Smith, William. "Intermittent Eye Malfunction and Their Effect on Reading." The Reading Teacher, 37(March 1984): 570-576.

THE PHYSICALLY HANDICAPPED CHILD WITH RELATED LANGUAGE DISABILITIES

Edelsky, Carole, and T.J. Rosegrant. "Language Development for Mainstreamed Severely Handicapped Non-Verbal Children." Language Arts, 58(January 1981): 68-76.

THE DISADVANTAGED OR DISABLED LEARNER

Chall, Jeanne, and Vicki Jacobs. "Writing and Reading in the Elementary Grades: Developmental Trends among Low SES Children." Language Arts, 60(May 1983): 617-616.

Ford, Michael, and Marilyn Ohlhausen. "Classroom Reading Incentive Programs: Removing the Obstacles and Hurdles for Disabled Readers." The Reading Teacher, 41(April 1988): 796-798.

Gaskins, Irene. "A Writing Program for Poor Readers and Writers and the Rest of the Class, Too." Language Arts, 59(November/December 1982): 854-861.

Hansen, Jane, and Ruth Hubbard. "Poor Readers Can Draw Inferences." The Reading Teacher, 37(March 1984): 586-589.

Herron, Naomi. "Three Motivators for Low-reading Sixth Graders." The Reading Teacher, 37(November 1983): 210-212.

Holbrook, Hilary. "ERIC/RCS Report: Motivating Reluctant Readers: A Gentle Push." Language Arts, 59(April 1982): 385-390.

Koenke, Karl. "Remedial Reading Instruction: What Is and What Might Be." The Reading Teacher, 41(March 1988): 708-711.

_____, and Jane McClellan. "ERIC/RCS Report: Teaching and Testing the Reading Disabled Child." Language Arts, 64(March 1987): 327-330.

Lanquetot, Roxanne. "Autistic Children and Reading." The Reading Teacher, 38(November 1984): 182-187.

Manzo, Anthony. "Psychologically Induced Dyslexia and Learning Disabilities." The Reading Teacher, 40(January 1987): 408-413.

Sinatra, Richard, Josephine Stahl-Gemake, and David Berg. "Improving Reading Comprehension of Disabled Readers Through Semantic Mapping." The Reading Teacher, 38(October 1984): 22-29.

Smith, Jeanne. "Writing in a Remedial Reading Program." Language Arts, 59(March 1982): 245-253.

Wagoner, Shirley. "The Portrayal of the Cognitively Disabled in Children's Literature." The Reading Teacher, 37(February 1984): 502-508.

THE GIFTED LEARNER

Carr, Kathryn. "What Gifted Readers Need from Reading Instruction." The Reading Teacher, 38(November 1984): 144-146.

Gitelman, Honre. "Motivating Accelerated Learners to Read." The Reading Teacher, 37(March 1984): 678-679.

Howell, Helen. "Language, Literature, and Vocabulary Development for Gifted Student." The Reading Teacher, 40(February 1987): 500-504.

Lukasevich, Ann. "Three Dozen Useful Information Sources on Reading for the Gifted." The Reading Teacher, 36(February 1983): 542-548.

May, Lola. "Teaching the Gifted Child." Early Years, 10(February 1980): 46-47.

Tway, Eileen. "The Gifted Child in Literature." Language Arts, 57(January 1980): 14-20.

IV. EXAMINATION QUESTIONS

A. Short Discussion Questions

1. There are three basic approaches to helping children who speak a nonstandard dialect. Make a data chart that describes each and gives its limitations.

2. One of a teacher's major responsibilities to exceptional children is _identification_ of individual learning needs and problems. Describe briefly two major ways through which you can meet this responsibility in your classroom.

3. Distinguish among the three kinds of articulation disorders: substitution, omission, and distortion.

4. List three behaviors that might indicate a possible hearing disorder; list three that might indicate a visual impairment.

5. Below are listed some techniques for working with speech-handicapped children. Next to each, indicate how that technique contributes to a child's speech development.
   a. Oral interpretation of literature selections.
   b. Informal conversations.
   c. Listening to stories and poems.

6. For each group of exceptional children listed below, describe four ways you should adjust your teaching to aid a child in language learning.
   a. Hearing impaired.
   b. Visually impaired.
   c. Slow learner.

7. _Open-book questions_: Reread the Teaching-in-Action episode at the beginning of Chapter 13. Then write an analysis of it in which you
   a. Describe the teaching strategies used.
   b. Note the objectives being sought.
   c. Suggest the assumptions about language learning on which the teacher is functioning.

B. Multiple-Choice Questions

1. Of the following, which is _not_ an accurate statement regarding instruction of children who are learning English as a second language?
   a. The teacher must serve as speech model in the second language for the children.
   b. The teacher must be able to speak the children's first language in order to facilitate second-language acquisition.
   c. The teacher must be aware of the child's cultural as well as language differences.
   d. The teacher must design sequences that focus on the major differences between first and second languages.

2. The term <u>bilingualism</u> when applied to educational programs means that
   a. Children are not required to learn a second language; they build fluency in their native language because it is so important to them.
   b. Children learn a second language and cease to function in their first, or native, language.
   c. Children acquire a second language while continuing in the development of their first language.
   d. All of the above, depending on the circumstances, the first language, and the ability level of the children.

3. With children who are language different, stress should initially be on
   a. Oral language.
   b. Spelling of the written language.
   c. Written language.
   d. Handwriting.
   e. Content-area learnings.

4. The word <u>standard</u> when applied to language usage refers to
   a. Superior forms of expression.
   b. Socially acceptable forms of expression.
   c. Correct forms of expression.
   d. British English.
   e. Black English.

5. Dialects differ from one another in
   a. Pronunciation, vocabulary, and syntax.
   b. Vocabulary and syntax.
   c. Vocabulary and pronunciation.
   d. Syntax.
   e. Syntax and pronunciation.

6. Your text recommends that a language development program for children who speak a nonstandard dialect should
   a. Be taught by a teacher who uses nonstandard dialect as the primary medium of classroom communication.
   b. Stress the written rather than the spoken language.
   c. Move from the written language into numerous oral experiences.
   d. Develop spoken vocabulary through extensive firsthand experiences.
   e. Help the child understand that his or her home dialect is inferior and should not be used in school.

7. Of the three approaches to teaching the dialectally different, most language arts specialists advocate the
   a. replace approach.
   b. keep approach.
   c. add approach.

8. According to Peterson's definition, slow learners are those who
   a. Are inattentive to class work.
   b. Have IQs between 85 and the high 90s.
   c. Cannot learn.
   d. Are generally taught in special education classrooms.
   e. Have difficulty in getting along with their classmates.

9. Which of the following strategies is (are) recommended for language-slow

learners?
a. More drill so that children learn mechanical operations.
b. More repetition of sight words.
c. More participation in reading-readiness activities.
d. More assistance in writing thoughts on paper.
e. All of the above.

10. Which of the following instructional strategies is (are) recommended for use with gifted children?
a. Considerable time spent in repetitive practice.
b. Emphasis on memory-level questions.
c. The fusing of reading and writing so that children learn to use diverse literary forms.
d. Encouragement of gifted children to follow the leadership of slower children.
e. All of the above.

11. Which of the following is an important question to ask in identifying a gifted child?
a. How rapidly does this child learn?
b. How friendly is this child?
c. How polite and well mannered is this child?
d. How attentive to class work is this child?
e. All of the above.

12. In teaching the hearing impaired to spell, the teacher may have to rely on
a. Tactile, kinesthetic, and visual techniques.
b. Linguistic approaches that stress sound-symbol relationships.
c. Visual and linguistic approaches rather than tactile and kinesthetic approaches.
d. Visual, tactile, and linguistic approaches rather than kinesthetic approaches.
e. Tactile and linguistic approaches rather than visual and kinesthetic approaches.

13. Which of the following can cause retarded speech development?
a. Overall mental retardation.
b. Hearing impairment.
c. Lack of speech stimulation.
d. Emotional shock.
e. All of the above.

14. In work with older children who already manifest secondary stuttering behavior, recommended techniques include
a. Urging students to speak more quickly or slowly.
b. Urging students to stop and start over.
c. Urging students to take a deep breath.
d. All of the above.
e. None of the above.

15. It is true to say that the techniques applicable in guiding the language learning of average learners are
    a. Never applicable in guiding the language learning of exceptional children.
    b. Of limited potential in working with exceptional children.
    c. Productive for use with exceptional children when the techniques are adapted to take into account differences in attention span, emotional level, and speed of learning.
    d. Applicable in the same way with exceptional children.

EXAMINATIONS

Reproduce these examinations to use as a midterm and a final.
These exams ask students to analyze, apply, plan, create, and
generalize, as well as explain and discuss what they have learned.

MIDTERM EXAMINATION

COMMUNICATION IN ACTION

Read the following Teaching-in-Action vignette. Then, in your examination booklet, write the answers to the questions that follow. Remember to plan your answers before beginning to write.

THE STORY LINE

All was quiet in the second-grade classroom. Every child's eyes were riveted on Barbara Schwartz, the teacher, for this was story time! "Once there was a fantastic maid named Amelia Bedelia who came to work for Mr. and Mrs. Rogers in a big house," began Ms. Schwartz, putting into her own words the popular story by Peggy Parish.

As the teacher introduced the tale, she took from a basket sitting on the floor a sizable piece of blue construction paper imprinted with the name of the story and its author. With a clothespin she clipped this title sheet to the far end of a length of plastic clothesline she had strung across the room. Resuming the story, Ms. Schwartz recounted Amelia's first meeting with the Rogerses and told how Mrs. Rogers gave Amelia a list of tasks to do since she and Mr. Rogers were going out. At this point Ms. Schwartz again reached into the basket and took from it a piece of yellow construction paper bearing the label "LIST" and containing all the items on Mrs. Rogers's story list. Ms. Schwartz clipped this item to the line next to the title piece.

Continuing the story, Ms. Schwartz described Amelia's reaction to the Rogerses' big house; at the same time she reached into her basket to pull out another piece of construction paper, this one red and shaped like the house in the book. She clipped the house to the story line as the second-graders inched forward in their seats to hear and see what she would say and do next.

As the story unfolded, Barbara Schwartz continued to add piece after piece to the line. By the time she had told the whole story, the line was filled with a paper lemon-meringue pie, light bulb, dusting powder canister, chicken, steak, drapes, and other pieces related to story events. When she read the last line, which indicates that Amelia Bedelia got to keep her job with the Rogerses, the children broke into spontaneous applause.

Now the teacher called for volunteers to retell the story of the literally minded maid and simultaneously to remove the pieces from the story line. Boys and girls eagerly came forward. As each in turn removed a colored shape, he or she retold the event associated with that shape. Children who had not participated in this retelling asked if they could hang the story again. This they did, repeating it in their own words.

Afterward, the youngsters paired off as conversation mates to talk informally about the story. Each member of a pair was to share with his or her mate a favorite part, explaining why he or she particularly liked that section. Each was to be prepared to tell the whole class the part chosen by the mate and the reason for the choice.

The quiet attention of story time was replaced by a cacophony of voices. Once the teacher had to strike a chord on the piano to gain attention. She reminded the class that in conversing, voices should be kept low; she also reminded the children to listen with care so that they could relate what they were being told.

Conversation time was short. Children regrouped to share. Presenters were able to retell the part chosen by their mates. The reasons for the choices, however, were less clear, with statements such as "It was funny" or "It was silly" prevailing.

On successive days, Ms. Schwartz's second-graders worked in groups to concoct original stories to replace Amelia Bedelia on the story line. Children cut out colored pieces and at times added words to the pieces to go along with the stories they were composing. Later, they orally shared their stories with listening classmates as they hung their story pieces on the line. After stories had been shared, listeners "celebrated" the writing by talking about their favorite parts.

QUESTIONS

1. What basic beliefs about language arts instruction undergird Ms. Schwartz's lesson sequence with Amelia Bedelia? For each belief you give, indicate that segment of the lesson which shows that Ms. Schwartz is functioning in terms of the belief.

2. What were Ms. Schwartz's objectives in teaching the lesson? For each objective you list, state what Ms. Schwartz did to achieve her objective. In other words, state the specific activity she planned to realize her objective.

3. Explain one way you might modify Ms. Schwartz's lesson to make it more effective.

4. Describe three additional activities that Ms. Schwartz could have used as part of the lesson sequence, or as follow-up to the sequence. State the objective(s) of each of these activities.

5. Write a literature-based plan for an upper-grade lesson modeled after Ms. Schwartz's lesson. Use a specific children's book as the basis for your plan. Be sure that your plan is in line with the beliefs you set forth in question 1, that you state your objectives, and that you include creative strategies to involve children in oral-language activity.

6. Educators are learning more and more about children's development as language users and thinkers. Write several paragraphs in which you explain children's growth as language users and thinkers. Be sure to include these terms in your explanation: assimilation, accommodation, schema, inner speech, expansion, and reduction.

FINAL EXAMINATION

COMMUNICATION IN ACTION

Read the following Teaching-in-Action vignette. Then, in your examination booklet, write the answers to the questions that follow. Remember to plan out your answers before beginning to write.

CITY AS MACHINE

Henry Dag welcomed his sixth-graders one afternoon with a marquee that announced:

The Creative Thinking Forge

Enter here to hammer out ideas.
 Equipment necessary:
  Hammer to shape ideas.
  Anvil to bang ideas on.
  Forge to heat up ideas so they are malleable.
  Mental tongs to grab ideas as you shape them.
Filmstrip viewing: The City at 1:00 P.M.
Forging session following the viewing!

This afternoon, the filmstrip projector and tape recorder were on standby, and Mr. Dag treated the class to a viewing of the full-color sound filmstrip The City. The strip has no narration and, through sounds and pictures, helps students perceive the variety and beauty of an urban environment. Mr. Dag used the filmstrip to immerse students in city things and thoughts as part of a module on urban living.

Sparking Creative Relationships

When the students had viewed the two nine-minute segments that constitute the strip, Mr. Dag explained that they were going to forge some new relationships. He sparked thinking by asking: "Have you ever thought of a city as a big machine? In what ways is a city like a machine?" First responses were words that could describe the workings of both city and machine. To spark more comparisons, the teacher interjected ideas to consider: "Think of things shared by cities and machines. Think of -ing words that describe both machine and city actions. Think of how city and machine are at the beginning of the day and at the end of the day. Think of words that tell 'when.'" As pupils responded, Mr. Dag recorded items on a city-as-machine chart:

137

THE CITY AS MACHINE

Is	Is	Has	Runs	Is
big, giant,	in action,	lots of	day and	running,
noisy,	in motion,	moving	night, every	turning,
mighty,	in a hurry	parts: gears,	hour, any	roaring,
dirty, busy,		joints,	hour, all the	grinding,
beautiful,		rollers, nuts	time, now,	turning,
heavy,		and bolts,	then,	halting,
monstrous		shuttles,	yesterday	spinning,
		wheels	and	starting up
			tomorrow	

From these words, the sixth-graders together hammered out a free thought--
"City Machine":

City Machine

The mighty city runs all day--
  Roaring loudly,
  Grinding fast,
  Pounding more,
  Spinning round.

The mighty city runs all night--
  Roaring softly,
  Grinding slowly,
  Pounding less,
  Spinning on.

At that point Mr. Dag encouraged students to forge new relationships,
asking them: "Do you think a city is more like a tree, a beehive, or a
carousel?" He distributed contemplation slips: scraps of colored paper. Each
sixth-grader picked one of the three options, wrote the option on his or her
contemplation slip, and added a few notes on ways the chosen item resembles a
city. On the slip, too, each youngster wrote words usually associated with a
tree, a beehive, or a carousel that could be applied to a city as well.

Having contemplated the options, the students orally expressed their
choices, which were about evenly distributed among the three options. This
difference of opinion stimulated talk, and youngsters willingly volunteered
reasons for selecting a particular option. Again by asking questions, Mr. Dag
encouraged students to explore their reasons. For example, he asked young
people developing the analogy between a tree and a city: "In what way can we
say that a city has roots? branches? leaves? Are there seasonal tree words that
we can use in talking about a city?"

Interestingly, the teacher had to ask few questions, for the preliminary
work with city as machine had laid the groundwork; students understood what
kinds of relationships to explore. As the class shared words and ideas, a

scribe recorded on the board words related to the object in question that could be applied to a city. The final list looked something like the one here:

METAPHORS FOR THE CITY

Beehive Words		Tree Words		Carousel Words	
buzzing	humming	grows	spreads	up and down	music
noisy	bees	roots	leaves	around and around	spinning
busy	nonstop	branches	pointing	noisy	sounds
tight	crowded	arteries	veins	colored lights	moving
packed	jammed	network	intertwining	calling	rotating
moving	constant	interlacing	twisting	stops for people	
action	active	changing	moving	good times	
activity	building	swaying	rests	lots of people	
sweet	hive	waits for	cold cycles	flashing colors	
cells	makes	spring		dancing	
produces	comb				
occupied	many				

Writing and Reading Together and Alone

Forging sentences from the words, the children orally composed a series of similes. The ones they compromised on were "The city buzzes like a noisy beehive crowded with working bees"; "The city spreads like a growing tree sending out subway roots and highway branches"; and "The city moves like a friendly carousel going round and round, up and down."

By now the sixth-graders were in high gear; they brainstormed other things to which they could compare a city: a turtle, an escalator, a train, a planet, a bird, a pied piper, an anthill, a spider web. Working in cooperative teams, students created comparisons based on their brainstormed lists. Shortly, they regrouped as a class so that the teams could share their comparisons.

During the week that followed, students edited their own writings to incorporate creative comparisons. During that week, too, as they read novels independently, they kept a pen in hand to record any creative comparisons they encountered. Later, as students shared their writings with one another, they listened for creative comparisons that struck their fancy.

QUESTIONS

1. What basic beliefs about language arts instruction undergird Mr. Dag's lesson sequence with creative comparisons? For each belief you give, indicate that segment of the lesson which supports the underlying belief.

2. What were Mr. Dag's objectives in teaching the lesson? For each objective you list, state what Mr. Dag did to achieve his objective. In other words, state the specific activity he planned to realize his objective.

3. Mr. Dag's lesson could be considered the rehearsal phase of a writing process sequence. Discuss in detail what it means to involve children in the

writing process. Include in your answer a discussion of:

o The stages of the writing process.
o The essence of each stage.
o Activities that are helpful at each stage.

4. Mr. Dag did not teach children specific usage, spelling, or handwriting skills as part of his lesson sequence. How does the teacher help children improve writing skills as part of the writing process? Include in your discusion consideration of spelling, handwriting, and usage skills.

5. Today, educators believe that young children should be involved in writing as soon as they enter school.

   a. Describe the stages that seem to characterize young children's development as writers.

   b. Explain ways to involve nursery and kindergarten children in the writing process. Draw on your understanding of language experience and whole-language approaches in developing your explanation.

6. Today, educators believe that making meaning is what reading is all about.

   a. What determines the meanings readers make as they read?

   b. How can a classroom teacher help children make meaning through reading? In answering this question, develop at least three major points.

APPENDIX A

SUGGESTED SYLLABUSES FOR LANGUAGE ARTS METHODS COURSES

I. A SYLLABUS FOR A LANGUAGE ARTS STRATEGIES COURSE WITH A WEEKLY SEMINAR
    SESSION THAT EXTENDS FOR APPROXIMATELY TWO AND ONE-QUARTER HOURS AND
    WHOSE PARTICIPANTS ARE CURRENTLY WORKING AS TEACHERS OR TEACHER-INTERNS

(Specific ideas for sessions suggested in the syllabus are detailed in the
individual chapters of this guide.)

Course title _____ Course number_____

Semester _____ Year _____ Room _____ Hours_____

Instructor _____

Instructor's office _____ Office phone _____

Instructor's office hours _____

A. Text for the Course

Hennings, Dorothy Grant. <u>Communication in Action: Teaching the Language Arts</u>,
fourth edition (Boston: Houghton Mifflin, 1990). Other basic readings: recent
issues of <u>Language Arts</u>, the journal of the National Council of Teachers of
English; and of <u>The Reading Teacher</u>, the journal of the International Reading
Association.

B. Tentative Sequence of Course Sessions

SESSION	IN-CLASS ACTIVITY	OUT-OF-CLASS ACTIVITY
1	a. A brief introduction to course design and requirements. b. A languaging-together session based on <u>The Girl Who Loved Wild Horses</u>. c. An analysis of the language-literature experience to identify language learnings, assumptions about instruction, and planning techniques.	Begin reading the first three chapters of your text and the preface.

SUGGESTED SYLLABUSES FOR LANGUAGE ARTS METHODS COURSES

SESSION	IN-CLASS ACTIVITY	OUT-OF-CLASS ACTIVITY
2	a. Looking at language: analyzing Ms. Morris's strategies. b. Reviewing theories about language learning and development.	Read Chapter 2 of your text in detail. Be prepared to share your findings, using a data-retrieval chart as an aid.
3	a. Looking at literature: analyzing books together. b. Participating in a literature-art laboratory based on a story (<u>The Rooster Who Set Out to See the World</u>.)	During the week, devise and set up a language-literature learning center in your class-room where children go as follow-up to a languaging-together time.
4	a. A sharing laboratory: learning centers in the language arts classroom.	Bring in your classroom learning center and the products children produced there. Be prepared to describe orally how your center functions.
5	a. Experiencing oral language: an activity laboratory where you will experience directly such techniques as drawing a story, pantomime, a participation story, and oral story composition. b. Designing listening experiences with stories: a work session.	Begin reading Chapters 4 through 7 of your text. Experiment with some of the activities in your classroom, especially experiences with b. stories and choral speaking. Bring to class a story or poem that you believe will serve as a profit-able springboard into listening and speaking.
6	a. Valuing together: a group exper-ience with oral approaches to values clarification. b. Designing together: a workshop in which participants design a session inclusive of some brainstorming and pondering experiences.	Begin work in your classroom on integrat-ing language learnings. Using a flow chart, plot a sequence of language activities that you could develop with children in your classroom over two to three weeks.

SESSION	IN-CLASS ACTIVITY	OUT-OF-CLASS ACTIVITY
7	Conferences with the instructor to discuss your plan for a two- to three-week sequence of language experiences with your students. Include small-group, class and personalized activities.	Bring your flow chart for individual conferencing. Finish reading Chapters 8 through 13 of your text.
8	a. Creating together: a creative writing workshop in which you will get a feel for creating. b. Discussion of problems encountered as you try out ideas in classroom settings.	Start your language learning sequence with your class of students.
9	a. "On a Yellow Ball Afternoon": an oral skills session followed by analysis. b. Designing together: putting together a spelling lesson based on an inductive scheme.	Continue your language learning sequence with your class of students.
10	a. Up the reading ladder: projecting questions that carry children up the ladder of cognition. b. Composing as a group: an experience with modeling. c. Discussion of your problems as you try ideas in classroom settings.	Continue your language learning sequence in your class. If you haven't done so already, finish reading your text and begin to read a book on language learning.
11	a. Language and linguistics: a brief presentation by the instructor. b. A sharing workshop: activities for teaching language.	Bring to class an activity--including teaching materials--through which you can involve children in some aspect of their language.
12	a. Looking at language differences. b. Modifying a language arts program to meet the needs of the exceptional student--a brief presentation by a specialist in the area.	Read an article on the language-different. Be prepared to share your findings, using a Note Card.

SESSION	IN-CLASS ACTIVITY	OUT-OF-CLASS ACTIVITY
13	A detailed sharing session: one-third of the class will describe the two- to three-week sequence of activities with language that they have developed in their classrooms.	
14	Same as Session 13.	
15	Same as Session 13.	
16	a. Developing a theory of language instruction: a round-table discussion of major issues, assumptions, plans, and strategies in which participants share ideas and develop a concept of what is involved in teaching the language arts successfully. b. Evaluation through individual conferences or testing.	

C. Detailed Description of Assignments

1. Read the text during the first half of the course. Select and read one additional book from the bibliographies contained at the ends of text chapters.

2. Develop a learning center in your classroom where youngsters go individually or in groups to participate in language activities. Bring your idea to class during Session 4 and be ready to share it orally with other participants. Have a one-page description of your center ready to distribute. As a result of the session in class, you should have several ideas for developing learning center with children.

3. Read Chapters 2 and 10 of your text in detail. Then create an activity or activity sequence for involving children with some aspect of their language. Be prepared to share your creation in Session 11.

4. Read a short journal article on teaching the dialectally different. The article should have appeared after 1980. Sources include Language Arts, The Reading Teacher, English Journal, Elementary School Journal, Instructor, and Learning. On a five-by-eight index card, write out key points from the article. Be prepared to share thoughts on the article orally during Session 12.

5. For the major project assignment for presentation during the final weeks of

the semester, plan and carry out a two- to three-week series of experience to involve children in a combination of language experiences. Include experiences that involve children with both oral and written language and that involve children individually, in small groups, and as a class. Try to devise an original game as part of your series. In upper grades particularly, integrate language experience into content-area learnings. You will be required to hand in:

    a.   A description of the activities you developed, including a flow chart that shows schematically just what happened.

    b.   A statement of assumptions underlying just what you did. This statement should be documented through reference to readings you have been completing in Language Arts, The Reading Teacher, and The Advocate.

    c.   Samples of children's work completed in reaction to the sequence.

You will also be asked to report orally on your project. You should be able to explain what you did, your assumptions, and the results. You may wish to show samples of children's work, materials you used, and your flow chart of activities.

II.   A SYLLABUS FOR A LANGUAGE ARTS STRATEGIES COURSE WITH TWO SESSIONS SCHEDULED EACH WEEK, EACH EXTENDING FOR ONE HOUR OR ONE HOUR AND FIFTEEN MINUTES. PARTICIPANTS NEED NOT BE TEACHING OR INTERNING. THE FIRST SESSION OF THE WEEK MAY BE FOR A LARGE GROUP, THE SECOND FOR A SMALLER GROUP OF THIRTY OR FEWER PARTICIPANTS.*

Course title _____ Course number _____

Semester _____ Year _____ Room _____ Hours _____

Instructor _____

Instructor's office _____ Office phone _____

Instructor's office hours _____

A.   Text for the Course

Hennings, Dorothy Grant. Communication in Action: Teaching the Language Arts, fourth edition (Boston: Houghton Mifflin Co., 1990). Other basic readings: recent issues of Language Arts, the journal of the National Council of Teachers of English; and of The Reading Teacher, the journal of the International Reading Association.

_____

*Specific ideas for each small-group session included in the syllabus are detailed in the individual chapters of this guide.

SUGGESTED SYLLABUSES FOR LANGUAGE ARTS METHODS COURSES

B. Tentative Sequence of Course Sessions

Topics and/or formats for each session are noted in the appropriate blocks;
assignments for which you are responsible are shown underscored and will be
described in greater detail under C (Course Requirements).

WEEK OF COURSE	FIRST SESSION OF WEEK (Small group)	SECOND SESSION OF WEEK (Large group)
1	Introduction: Languaging with literature, a firsthand experience in the language arts. Read Preface and Chapter 1 of the text.	Ways children learn language. Reading Chapter 2 of the text.
2	Experiencing literature and language in learning stations: you will look at some of the audio-visual materials that accompany books.	Books we share with younger children to encourage reading and to use as springboards into language experiences.
3	Experiencing literature and language in learning stations: you will try out story-sharing techniques by using flannelboards set up in learning stations.	Analyzing together: books to which older children respond--controversial books in the elementary school. Read Chapter 3 of the text.
4	Pondering together: a value-clarification laboratory in which we will experience teaching strategies directly. Read Chapter 7 of the text.	Listening and speaking activities in the content areas; an instructor presentation. Read Chapters 4 and 5 of the text.
5	Involvement laboratory; pantomiming, choral speaking, fingerplays, and impromptu dramatics--we will do them all. Assignment A is due today.	Story-sharing techniques demonstrated by the instructor and by Bill Cosby in the film Rich Cat, Poor Cat. Read Chapter 6.

WEEK OF COURSE	FIRST SESSION OF WEEK (Small group)	SECOND SESSION OF WEEK (Large group)
6	Drama festival 1. Assignment B is due today for half the class.	Organizing the classroom for instruction: film-showing of Primary Education in England.
7	Drama festival 2. Assignment B is due today for the other half of the class.	Examination.
8	Creative thinking-writing workshop: we will create a little prose and poetry. Read Chapter 8 of the text.	An instructor presentation on "Creativity: What Is It?"
9	A Yellow Ball Afternoon: a first-hand experience with languaging together and with generalizing about the outcomes. Read Chapter 9 of the text.	Individual conferences to consider problems/progress to date.
10	Sentencing and writing: a creating-teaching-materials lab on ways to develop sentence sense.	Thinking and writing: ways to encourage children to relate and to sequence. a. Brainstorming facts. b. Building storymaps.
11	Grammar: a sharing workshop. Assignment C is due today.	Usage and expression: a few techniques with opportunity for story reconstruction. Read Chapter 10 of the text.
12	Looking at language arts programs: an analytical session in which we study the emphases found in language arts text series.	Language history: an instructor presentation.

WEEK OF COURSE	FIRST SESSION OF WEEK	SECOND SESSION OF WEEK
13	Spelling/the encoding process: designing and sharing inductive lesson sequences. This will be a team-working-together lab.	Handwriting: one or two model lessons analyzing the episodes given in the text. <u>Read Chapter 11 of the text</u>.
14	Designing questions and activities to move children up the cognition ladder: another team-working-together lab. <u>Assignment E is due today</u>.	Reading/the decoding process: analyzing assumptions, goals, and strategies. <u>Read Chapter 12 of the text</u>.
15	A seminar discussion session on the language-different. <u>Assignment D is due today</u>.	Special children in the regular classroom: a presentation by a guest speaker. <u>Read Chapter 13 of the text</u>.
16	Putting it together: sharing ideas carried out as part of Assignment E. What are the goals of language arts instruction? How do we achieve these goals? <u>Read Concluding Section, Review of text</u>.	<u>Examination or individual conferences</u>.

C. Course Requirements

Assignment A. Selecting literature and using it as a springboard into language experience

Do either 1 or 2.

1. <u>Lower-grade teachers</u>. Select six picture storybooks. Read and compile an annotated bibliography listing the six books. Then select <u>one</u> of the six and write a short critical reaction to it, considering aspects described in Chapter 3 of your text. In this part of the paper, do not retell the story but critically analyze it. Next, describe a literature-language experience of your own creation in which you use the chosen book as a springboard into language activity.

2. <u>Upper-grade teachers</u>. Select three books for young people in upper grades. Read and compile an annotated bibliography listing the three books. Then select <u>one</u> and proceed as detailed under 1 above.

Assignment B. Dramatizing as oral expression

Each participant will perform in an activity related to pantomime, puppetry, creative dramatics, or storytelling, as part of one of two class drama festivals scheduled during the seventh and eighth weeks of the semester. By the fifth week, be prepared to tell the instructor:
1. The name of the story or poem you intend to share.
2. The colleagues with whom you intend to work if not sharing individually.
3. The form your sharing will take--puppets, objects, tapes, and so forth.

Assignment C. Creating ideas for teaching and sharing

Each participant will create an activity for involving children in some aspect of language--usage, grammar, or history. Prepare all the necessary materials for the activity. Describe the activity on one page that you duplicate and distribute as you describe the activity orally to your colleagues in a class-sharing session during the twelfth week of the semester.

Assignment D. Sharing ideas encountered in reading

Read a short journal article on teaching the dialectally different. The article read should be dated later than 1982 and should be drawn from <u>Language Arts</u>, <u>The Reading Teacher</u>, <u>The English Journal</u>, <u>Elementary School Journal</u>, <u>Instructor</u>, <u>Teacher</u>, or <u>Learning</u>. On a five-by-eight Note Card, record key points from the article read. Be ready to present ideas in class, using your card as a guide. Also be prepared to hand in your card.

Assignment E. Teaching

Prepare an activity--for a class, as a learning station, or as a one-to-one experience--for stimulating children to write stories, poetry, reactions, letters, or reports. Use this activity with a group of children you bring together for the occasion--or in a classroom, if you have access to one. Then write a brief paper in which you (a) describe what you did, (b) detail the assumptions underlying what you did, and (c) evaluate the results. Affix to your paper several representative samples of children's work produced in response to the activity. On the first page of the paper, indicate the age and grade level of each student, the number of children participating, and the source of your idea.

APPENDIX B

TASK SHEETS FOR LEARNING STATIONS IN
LANGUAGE ARTS METHODS COURSES

I. LEARNING-STATION TASK SHEET: ANALYZING SOUND FILMSTRIPS THAT
    ACCOMPANY PICTURE STORYBOOKS

A. Information

Many companies produce and sell sound filmstrips based on stories. Today you
will have the opportunity to examine one such audiovisual material and react to
it.

B. Purpose

To develop a heightened understanding of the ways to use audiovisual materials
related to storybooks.

C. Directions

1. Place the story tape in the tape recorder and the filmstrip in the viewer.
As the tape and strip tell the story, follow along in the book version you will
find at the station.

2. With team members, discuss the following questions; then individually
complete the Reaction Sheet by writing answers directly on it.

Reaction Sheet   Sound Filmstrips   Name_____

a. Is the text on the tape an exact duplicate of the text in the book?
    Why do you think this was done?
b. What is the source of the pictures found on the strip?
    Why do you think this was done?
c. One generalization important in using the sound filmstrip of a book is to
    have the book itself also available. Why is this a good instructional
    principle?
d. Do you think a filmstrip such as this one adds to or subtracts from
    enjoyment of the story? Explain your answer.
e. It is possible to use this type of sound filmstrip as the core of a
    learning station for students even beyond the primary years, in grades 3-5.
    Describe one activity set up as a learning station that you could develop
    with the filmstrip for older children. Then describe one activity for use

with primary children. Write your descriptions on the reverse side of the
Reaction Sheet.

II.   LEARNING-STATION TASK SHEET: USING FLANNELBOARDS TO SHARE STORIES

A. Information

To tell a flannelboard story, teachers or children can:
1. Use ready-made, precut story pieces that can be purchased through Hammet
Supply House, Vaux Hall Road, Union, NJ 07083.
2. Cut pieces from construction paper, spraying the back with glitter,
sticking strips of sandpaper on the back, or sticking strips of felt tape or
wads of masking tape to the back. This results in a rough-back surface that
adheres to the flannelboard.
3. Cut pieces from felt or flannel.

Clues on flannelboard use include:
1. Keep flannelboard at a good slant to prevent pieces from slipping.
2. Use a lightweight board that you and your students can manipulate easily.
Beware of very heavy boards that are hard to move.
3. If you like, get a board that can be turned over to become a pocket chart.
Pocket charts are great for linguistic studies.
4. Try to involve children in the storytelling right from the beginning, if
possible.
5. Use sound effects and vocal changes to add to the storytelling.

B. Purpose

Flannelboards can be used by:
1. Teachers, to share stories with young children.
2. Children, to share stories they have read or written with other children
(upper-grade youngsters can tell stories to lower-graders).

C. Directions

You will find several packets of story pieces. Each plastic packet contains
the pieces to use in telling a story. Take a packet of pieces, and read the
story outline found in the packet.
   Divide into subgroups of two. Each person in turn should tell the story
in a packet to his or her story partner. Try not to read the story. Tell it
from knowledge of the story outline. Improvise lines. Try to involve the
listener in the storytelling.
   After each has shared a story with another, select three or four pieces
from the box of miscellaneous flannel shapes. Use those pieces to invent a
story on the spot.

152

III. LEARNING-STATION TASK SHEET: ANALYZING COMMERCIALLY PREPARED MATERIALS
      FOR USE IN INDIVIDUALIZING

A. Information

Today there is a wealth of commercially prepared materials available that you
can use as the basis for a learning-station activity. Some of these materials
have been specifically designed for use in learning stations. Other materials
can be easily adapted so that children can use the materials independently to
build language facility.

B. Purpose

To analyze commercially available materials that can be the base of independent
learning activity and to think about how to use the materials.

C. Directions

1. Systematically examine materials set out at this station, and record your
evaluation of each material on the following chart.

Title of material and source from which to obtain it	Ability of material to stimulate creative thinking excellent good fair poor	Usefulness for independent study in stations excellent good fair poor
1.		
2.		
3.		
4.		
5.		

2. As a group, select a material that was not designed specifically for use in
an independent learning station. Decide how you could use it as a way of
stimulating independent language activity. Write a description of how your
group would use the material on this sheet. Keep the sheet as part of your own
repertoire of notes for the course.

APPENDIX C

PROBLEMS TO FOCUS SMALL-GROUP DISCUSSIONS
IN LANGUAGE ARTS METHODS COURSES

Below is a series of error-ridden language learning sequences. Any one can be typed onto a discussion Task Sheet, and pre- and in-service teachers can identify the weaknesses incorporated in it. Or these problems can be made part of a final evaluation in which college students react to the problems and propose alternate lesson designs.

Problem 1: The fifth-grade class had ben studying haikus and cinquains for several days. The class had identified the structure of these forms by studying several examples of each; the children had written pieces as a teacher-guided group and in small groups. At that point the teacher asked the children to compose a haiku independently. Paul composed this piece: "Dandelion flowers/blow in the breeze . . . Little airplanes/flying round and round." Following the writing, the teacher had each child illustrate his or her piece and then share it with the class. Students listened to see whether the piece followed the haiku pattern. When Paul shared his piece with the class, his classmates quickly picked up that it was not in the common haiku syllable pattern. The teacher tactfully suggested to Paul that he redo his piece to make it fit the 5-7-5 syllable pattern of the haiku. What are the strengths and weaknesses of this lesson sequence?

Problem 2: The second-grade teacher began her lesson by dictating to the children the generalizations about the hard and soft sounds of the g and the vowels that follow the g. She instructed the children to write the generalizations in their notebooks. Then she had them copy from their spelling book those words which begin with a soft g and those which begin with a hard g. She had the children search through magazines to find and cut out pictures to go with the word listed. Later she read aloud other words that begin with g. The children listened and decided whether the g was soft or hard. What are the strengths and weaknesses of the lesson?

Problem 3: A third-grade teacher decided to do more with written expression. He therefore spent several half-hour sessions helping children to pick out the noun phrases and verb phrases in sentences that he presented to the class with the overhead projector. He had the children come forward to circle the noun phrases and to underline the verb phrases being projected. At that point, with this preparation, he told the class, "You now know how to write a sentence with noun phrases and verb phrases. I want you to write a very short story about a monkey who liked bananas. Remember to write sentences with noun phrases and verb phrases." What problems do you see in his lesson design?

Problem 4: An eighth-grade teacher decided that she wanted to teach children in her class how to prepare and present a formal speech. The topic of the speech was "The Most Exciting Thing That Ever Happened to Me." She began by telling the class how to write an outline for the speech; in doing so she emphasized the importance of a striking beginning, the need for fundamental facts in the middle, and the importance of a dynamic ending. Then she had the students write an outline for their speeches. Following the creation of the outlines, she had the students write out their speeches in paragraph form, using their outlines as guides. When the students had completed their papers, she suggested that they take them home and read them aloud several times. The next day the students took turns reading their speeches from their papers. What problems do you see in this lesson?

Problem 5: A fourth-grade teacher introduced a new topic in science--a rather complicated one with lots of new vocabulary words--by having the children silently read that portion of the text which applied to the topic. The teacher followed the reading with writing; the students wrote sentences that answered the questions found at the end of the section of the text. Later the children orally shared their answers in a round-table discussion. What problems do you see in the design of the lesson? How would you restructure it to make it a more effective language-learning experience as well as a science-learning experience?

Problem 6: A first-grade teacher used a basal reading series as the main content through which to teach his young students to read. Each day the children, working in skills groups, took turns reading aloud a paragraph from the basal reading book. The teacher followed the reading with a discussion of the pictures and questions to check comprehension. Later the students returned to their seats to pursue other reading tasks; these tasks included completing exercises in the workbook, rereading the basal reader story, and drawing pictures to go with the story. These activities constituted the reading program in his first grade. What problems do you perceive in the way the teacher handled reading?

APPENDIX D

MATERIALS FOR LANGUAGE ARTS METHODS SESSIONS

A. Here is a drawing story, composed by two girls in the sixth grade, that you may wish to share orally and visually with teachers as an example of what young people of this age can do when fully motivated.

Story   Accompanying Drawing

    Once there were two children. One was named Oliver and one was named Otis. Because their names began with <u>O</u>'s their houses were in the shape of two <u>O</u>'s. The two houses looked like this:

    One day Oliver went over to Otis's house and said, "Let's go across the street and clean up the park. There is lots of litter there.

    "Okay," said Otis, "let's go!" So first they cleaned up the whole sitting area.

    And emptied out the three garbage pails.

    "Now let's clean up around the big round lake," said Oliver.
    "Fine," said Otis, "let's go!" So, they cleaned up the area around the lake.

157

Then they decided to clean up the four playground areas and plant grass there.

And then they cleaned up around the big slide. Now they were done cleaning the park.

- - - use pink

- - - use pink

When the mayor of their town heard of what they did, he called them up and said that Otis and Oliver could have anything they wanted because they did such a good job. "Well," they said, "we sure would like carpet in our houses!"
"Then you shall have it!" said the mayor. So Otis and Oliver got new carpet in their houses. (It was pink carpet!)

B. Below is a description of a morning spent in a sixth-grade classroom. You may duplicate and distribute it as a culminating take-home examination. Students in the course may respond in writing to the following related questions or be prepared to respond orally in a class discussion. Either way, a part of a concluding summary session in which participants develop their own theory of language arts instruction can be dedicated to an oral analysis of the session.

The Questions

1. What assumptions about language learning and instruction are inherent in this episode?
2. How does the teacher meet individual differences in learning in his classroom? In his scheme, what purpose was served by class instruction? by instruction in small groups?
3. Chart out the plan of Mr. Lewis's session, showing schematically the flow of activity in the class.
4. What evidence is there of integration of the language arts? of correlation with other subject areas?
5. What specific learning goal is the teacher trying to achieve?
6. What are the strong points of this teacher's approach? the weak points?

The Session

Working Together--8:40 A.M.-9:15 A.M. Youngsters coming into Mr. Lewis's sixth grade gathered together for a brief talk-and-sharing time consisting of the following:
1. A choral speaking led by five students who were working on oral interpretation of punctuation markers. A girl with a phonation problem was a member of this group.
2. A progress report by an interest group that had developed a questionnaire to survey school interest in having a mock presidential election. Classmates offered suggestions.

158

3. A current-events sharing and discussion entitled "Names in the News." Mattie shared a magazine clip about a rock star, Bret a newspaper item on a recent visit to the United States of the president of Italy.
4. A quick check by the teacher to determine if all individuals and groups knew how they would spend the next hour and a half. At this point, Jotting Books appeared; sixth-graders recorded a capsule description of how they would use their time.

The Basal Studies Group. For the next half-hour, as about two-thirds of the class worked independently, Mr. Lewis guided the Basal Studies Group. The group comprised five youngsters reading considerably below grade level and three whose first language was Spanish. Working as a teacher-led group, group members scanned the basal-reader story they had read independently the previous day and then reacted to Mr. Lewis's questions: Why did Robert feel unhappy? What word did the writer use to show that Robert was unhappy? At what point did you feel that Robert was going to be O.K. Mr. Lewis recorded on the board key vocabulary words that surfaced during the discussion and went back at the end of the discussion to have readers pronounce the words and talk about meaning and usage.

With the basal group, Mr. Lewis spent about ten minutes analyzing word relationships by converting nouns into adjectives. Children converted sentences such as "His legs were filled with bone" into "His legs were bony." As the teacher offered other sample sentences ("The room was filled with noise," "The bed was filled with bugs," "Her hair was a mess"), children rephrased them by producing an adjective form of the noun ("noisy," "buggy," "messy") and then listened for similarly formed words in "The Misty, Moisty Morning," which their teacher read aloud to them.

At that point, the eight figured out their work agenda for the remaining hour and the first half-hour of the reading-language period scheduled for the next day. They were to do the following:
1. Begin by completing an exercise providing practice with the suffix -y; read "The Teeny Tiny Woman" and see how -y words were used to add style to the story; and then move on to complete personalized activities outlined on their independent study agenda. Some of these activities would take them to learning stations in the room.
2. Use the remainder of the period to read in the book chosen during a recent library visit or write a repetitive -y story or poem.
3. Use the first half-hour of the next day to read a related story in the basal reader and think about how the feelings of the story character compared with Robert's feelings in the story just discussed.

The Political Systems Research Group. For the next half-hour, Mr. Lewis guided nine highly involved students whose reading levels ranged from ninth to twelfth grade. Spurred by an upcoming national election, they were researching the way governments differ in other countries. They had spent the first part of the period scanning and noting encyclopedia pages to locate significant facts that would show comparisons. On the previous day, each had searched to select a particular country for study--Japan, Russia, Sweden, Great Britain, and so forth. Working with their teacher, the researchers orally shared key passages from their encyclopedia volume to indicate what might be an important fact or generalization to include in the group's final oral presentation before the entire class. As a teacher-led group, they formulated key questions to aid in selecting material to include: How are top governmental leaders chosen? How long do leaders remain in power? How can leaders be thrown out? What freedoms do the people possess? Can the press write what it wants? The teacher helped with pronunciation of difficult words--<u>totalitarianism</u>, for example--and talked briefly about the concepts represented by the terms. The teacher also directed members to talk about the graphic means they could employ to share data with the class and what format for presentation would maintain listener interest.

As the group went back to organize Note Cards relevant to each question identified in the discussion, Mr. Lewis conferred briefly with one of the nine. Julie, a particularly gifted youngster, had ben reading <u>Watership Down</u>. She and Mr. Lewis discussed the allegorical meanings of the incidents she had already read. All the students in the group were reading books they had chosen, and each day for about five minutes Mr. Lewis would confer with one or two about reactions to what they were reading. To guide these fast readers, Mr. Lewis had prepared a form with such statements as "Think about: reasons for character actions; big ideas developed through the story incidents; ways the writer uses description, dialogue, and action to weave the story." As students read, they jotted down reactions, using one or two statements chosen from the form.

Leaving the group, Mr. Lewis commented, "This group has really been taking off. Keep it up, especially you, Bruce. You really helped today with the key points." Bruce, a brilliant but withdrawn boy, generally worked poorly with a group; he preferred to work on his own. Mr. Lewis also said, "Make sure to leave some time today and tomorrow to read in your library books. I'll be talking with Sue and Jane tomorrow about their personal reading."

<u>The Specialized Social Studies Skills Group</u>. Off Mr. Lewis went to meet with the Specialized Social Studies Skills Group, which for the first half-hour had been working at learning stations--two grouping social studies ideas into an outline; four sketching a time line from information gleaned from a sound filmstrip on the westward migration that was part of a history study in progress; two searching large maps of the West for interesting geographical names and hypothesizing reasons certain features received their names; and one outlining on the bulletin board a map of the United States that would be utilized eventually to plot patterns of westward migration.

For the next half-hour or so, group member had read to themselves a mimeographed story about the western migration that Mr. Lewis had distributed and introduced the previous day, when he and they had talked together and had analyzed the structure of such words as <u>disaster</u>, <u>hardship</u>, <u>endure</u>, <u>caravan</u>, and <u>irrepressible</u> that they would meet in the story. Now, during the last half-hour of the period, the group members talked with Mr. Lewis about motivation and about why the settlers were willing to endure hardships. Mr. Lewis suggested that either individually or in pairs they write hardship stories that were close enough to the fact to have actually happened-- historical fiction. This they would do first thing the next morning.

<u>The Questioners</u>. In the last ten minutes of the period, Mr. Lewis conferred with a special projects group comprising members from other groups in the room. This group was preparing to survey interest in a schoolwide presidential election. Two students agreed to prepare the edited questionnaire on a ditto master and take it to the office for duplication. They decided when and where they would distribute it and who would help them. They planned to announce their procedure during the general class session the next morning.

By then it was eleven o'clock. The sixth-graders were off to the gymnasium for physical activity with the gym teacher. Mr. Lewis sat down!

More Questions--A Bit More Difficult

1. How is this approach to teaching reading and the language arts similar to
    that of Ms. Wilkening in Chapter 12 of the text? How is it different?
    Consider:
    a. The language learnings being stressed.
    b. Differences and similarities in the use of personalized and small-
        group activity.
    c. Differences and similarities in basic assumptions about how to teach
        the language arts.
    d. Reasons for those differences and similarities.

2. Compare and contrast Mr. Lewis's approach with that described in the
    opening episode of your text in Chapter 2--"On a Yellow Ball Afternoon."
    Consider points a-d in this context.

APPENDIX E

ANSWER KEY FOR MULTIPLE-CHOICE TEST ITEMS

CHAPTER 1   TEACHING FOR COMMUNICATION--A NATURAL APPROACH TO THE
              LANGUAGE ARTS

              1. c   11. d
              2. d   12. a
              3. d   13. c
              4. a   14. c
              5. c   15. b
              6. a   16. b
              7. b   17. d
              8. d   18. b
              9. d   19. a
              10. e   20. c

CHAPTER 2   LANGUAGE AND CHILDREN'S LANGUAGE DEVELOPMENT--WHERE COMMUNICATION
              IS IN ACTION

              1. c   10. d   19. a
              2. a   11. b   20. d
              3. a   12. e
              4. b   13. d
              5. d   14. c
              6. c   15. b
              7. d   16. c
              8. a   17. c
              9. b   18. d

CHAPTER 3   LITERATURE IN THE LANGUAGE ARTS--WHERE CHILDHOOD'S DREAMS
              ARE TWINED

              1. b   9. c
              2. d   10. b
              3. e   11. a
              4. b   12. e
              5. d   13. d
              6. c   14. c
              7. c   15. d
              8. a

ANSWER KEY FOR MULTIPLE-CHOICE TEST ITEMS

CHAPTER 4   LISTENING FOR MEANING--LEARNING TO LISTEN AND LISTENING
              TO LEARN

              1. c   10. d
              2. c   11. c
              3. e   12. d
              4. b   13. a
              5. a   14. a
              6. c   15. b
              7. b
              8. b
              9. a

CHAPTER 5   ORAL COMMUNICATION--SHARING STORIES AND POEMS THROUGH
              CREATIVE ACTIVITY

              1. e
              2. b
              3. d
              4. b
              5. a
              6. e
              7. e

CHAPTER 6   ORAL COMMUNICATION--SHARING IDEAS THROUGH CONVERSING
              AND REPORTING

              1. d   10. b
              2. d
              3. a
              4. a
              5. d
              6. d
              7. c
              8. a
              9. c

CHAPTER 7   THINKING OUT LOUD--TALKING, LISTENING, WRITING, AND
              READING TOGETHER

              1. d   10. a
              2. a
              3. f
              4. d
              5. e
              6. c
              7. b
              8. b
              9. e

CHAPTER 8   WRITING AS IDEA MAKING--THOUGHT IN ACTION

1. c   10. a   18. b
2. c   11. c   19. d
3. c   12. b   20. c
4. a   13. a
5. e   14. a
6. d   15. a
7. a   16. b
8. d   17. b
9. d

CHAPTER 9   THE WRITING PROCESS--FUNCTIONING AS AN AUTHOR

1. d   10. a
2. a   11. c
3. a   12. e
4. a   13. a
5. d   14. a
6. e
7. c
8. b
9. b

CHAPTER 10   LANGUAGE PATTERNS, USAGE, AND GRAMMAR--MANAGING IDEAS

1. a   10. a
2. a   11. b
3. b   12. c
4. c   13. d
5. c
6. b
7. d
8. d
9. b

CHAPTER 11   SPELLING, DICTIONARY USE, AND HANDWRITING--TOOLS OF THE
             EDITOR'S CRAFT

1. e   10. d
2. b   11. e
3. a   12. a
4. c   13. d
5. a   14. c
6. e   15. c
7. a   16. a
8. a   17. e
9. b

ANSWER KEY FOR MULTIPLE-CHOICE TEST ITEMS

CHAPTER 12   READING FOR MEANING--LEARNING TO READ AND READING TO
             LEARN

1.	c	12.	d	23.	c
2.	a	13.	d	24.	d
3.	d	14.	d	25.	f
4.	a	15.	b	26.	a
5.	b	16.	c	27.	a
6.	a	17.	a	28.	e
7.	d	18.	b	29.	c
8.	f	19.	a	30.	b
9.	e	20.	d	31.	c
10.	b	21.	a	32.	d
11.	e	22.	c	33.	b

CHAPTER 13   CHILDREN WITH LANGUAGE DIFFERENCES AND DIFFICULTIES

1.	b	10.	c
2.	c	11.	a
3.	a	12.	a
4.	b	13.	e
5.	a	14.	e
6.	d	15.	c
7.	c		
8.	b		
9.	e		

APPENDIX F

INSTRUCTIONAL MASTERS

Use these Instructional Masters to make handouts and/or transparencies to go along with <u>Communication in Action</u>, Fourth Edition.

Communication in Action:

Teaching the Language Arts

TEACHING FOR COMMUNICATION:

A NATURAL APPROACH

TO THE LANGUAGE ARTS

	WHAT IT MEANS IN TERMS OF CLASSROOM ACTIVITY	ADVANTAGES/ DISADVANTAGES
BELIEF 1:		
BELIEF 2:		
BELIEF 3:		
BELIEF 4:		

HENNINGS, *COMMUNICATION IN ACTION*

❄ MS. TOPPING'S LESSON SEQUENCE ❄ WITH *ROSIE'S WALK*

SEQUENCE OF ACTIVITIES	WHAT THE ACTIVITY ACHIEVED
1. CHILDREN LISTEN TO *ROSIE'S WALK*.	
2. CHILDREN RETELL THE STORY.	
3.	

HENNINGS, *COMMUNICATION IN ACTION*

❄ MS. TOPPING'S LESSON SEQUENCE ❄ WITH THE WATER CYCLE	
SEQUENCE OF ACTIVITIES	**WHAT THE ACTIVITY ACHIEVED**
1. CHILDREN OBSERVED AND DESCRIBED AN ICE CUBE.	
2. CHILDREN DREW PICTURES OF THEIR OBSERVATIONS.	
3.	

HENNINGS, *COMMUNICATION IN ACTION*

◼◼◼ A Guide for Lesson Planning ◼◼◼

Topic of Lesson: **Grade Level:**

Context:

Proposed Sequence of Activities:

1. Anticipatory Set:

2. Instruction and Modeling:

3. Guided Practice (if necessary):

4. Closing Set:

5. Follow-up Independent Activity:

Materials:

Evaluation:

| BRAINSTORM THOUGHTS THAT COME TO MIND WHEN |
| YOU HEAR THE WORDS *PLAIN* AND *TALL*. |

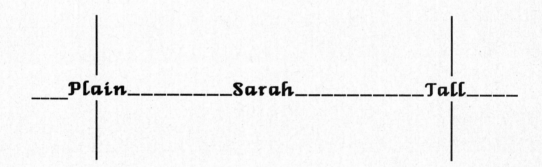

Story Characters	Kind of Person	Evidence from Story That Supports Our Inference
Caleb		
Anna		
Papa		
Sarah		

Language and Children's Language

Development:

Where Communication IS in Action

★★ THE YELLOW BALL AFTERNOON ★★

THE ACTIVITY	ASSUMPTIONS UNDER-LYING THE ACTIVITY
☆ CHORAL SPEAKING— PEASE PORRIDGE HOT	
☆ TALKING ABOUT PEASE PORRIDGE HOT	
☆ PLAYING WITH HOMOPHONES—PAIR, PARE, PEAR	
☆ PLAYING WITH ADJECTIVES & ADVERBS	
☆ REPORTING ON THE NEWS	
☆ WORKING INDEPENDENTLY	

HENNINGS, *COMMUNICATION IN ACTION*

DATA RETRIEVAL CHART—LANGUAGE DEVELOPMENT		
	Terms Associated with This Area	**Brief Summary of Key Points Relevant to the Topic**
1. Concept Formation		
2. Development of Communication and Thinking Power		
3. Development of Ability to Use Words		
4. Development of Ability to Handle Sentence Patterns		

HENNINGS, *COMMUNICATION IN ACTION*

Chapter 2, Master 3, cont.

	Terms Associated with This Area	Brief Summary of Key Points Relevant to the Topic
5. Development of Ability to Use and Interpret Vocal Intonation		
6. Development of Ability to Use and Interpret Nonverbal Language		

Conclusions: How do children learn to communicate?

HENNINGS, *COMMUNICATION IN ACTION*

☆☆☆☆☆☆☆☆☆☆☆☆☆☆☆☆☆☆☆☆☆☆☆☆

An Interactive Model of Early Language Development
from
Communication in Action

Parent talks ➡ ➡ ➡ ➡ ➡ ➡ ➡ Child imitates and
with child   ⬇   reduces parents'
              ⬇   sentences
              ⬇
              ⬇
              ⬇

Parent expands ⬅ ⬅ ⬅ ⬅ ⬅ Child speaks in
child's   ⬇   telegraphic
utterances   ⬇   sentences
              ⬇
              ⬇
              ⬇

Child internalizes "rules" for
sentence-making and uses them
intuitively during further interactions

HENNINGS, *COMMUNICATION IN ACTION*

Literature

in the Language Arts:

Where Childhood's Dreams Are Twined

✳✳✳✳✳✳✳✳✳✳✳✳✳✳✳✳✳✳✳✳✳✳✳✳✳✳✳✳✳

A Guide for Analyzing Feelings in Stories

Book Title: _____ Author: _____

✳ Strategy: Stop reading for a moment.
   On the guide, describe what is happening in the story.
   Decide: How does the character feel at this moment?
   Decide: How do you feel at this moment reading the
           story?
   Repeat the strategy for other events in the story.

Description of the Event:	How the Character Feels:	How You Feel:
1.		
2.		
3.		

HENNINGS, *COMMUNICATION IN ACTION*

✳✳✳✳✳✳✳✳✳✳✳✳✳✳✳✳✳✳✳✳✳✳✳✳✳✳✳✳✳

A Prediction Guide

Title: _____   Author: _____

✳ **Strategy:** Stop reading for a moment.
Predict what is going to happen next to a character.
Write the name of the character and your prediction
on the guide.
Write down the story clues to support your prediction.

Character:	Prediction— What Is Going to Happen:	The Clues That Support the Prediction:
1.		
2.		
3.		
4.		

HENNINGS, *COMMUNICATION IN ACTION*

✳✳ STORY ELEMENTS ✳✳

CHARACTERISTICS OF A STORY	SIGNIFICANCE OF THE CHARACTERISTIC
✳ SETTING	
✳ CHARACTERS	
✳ PLOT	
✳ THEME	
✳ VERBAL STYLE	
✳ CONCLUSIONS: WHAT MAKES A GOOD STORY?	

HENNINGS, *COMMUNICATION IN ACTION*

✳ PLOT PATTERNS IN STORIES ✳

KIND OF PATTERN	EXAMPLE OF STORY	DESCRIPTION OF STORY
✳ STEP BY STEP		
✳ TURN ABOUT		
✳ CIRCULAR		
✳ JUST IMAGINE		
✳ CONCLUSIONS: WHY IS A KNOWLEDGE OF STORY PATTERNS HELPFUL TO A STORY READER?		

HENNINGS, *COMMUNICATION IN ACTION*

Listening for Meaning:

Learning to Listen and

Listening to Learn

❋ **Discussion Guide** ❋

❋ **Getting at the Root of Conflict** ❋

1. **What was Ms. Arnold's anticipatory set? What do you think she hoped to achieve by beginning in this way?**

2. **Why do you think the teacher read the introductory section of the text, indicating as she went along the thoughts that came to her mind?**

3. **Why do you think the teacher showed the students the headings within the text and asked them to make up questions to keep in mind as they listened to each subsection?**

---

4. Why do you think the teacher asked the children to create a web before listening?

5. How did Ms. Arnold structure the time after the children had listened to the selection on conflict? What was she hoping to achieve?

6. At what point were the students involved in critical rather than informational thinking?

7. Why did Ms. Arnold have the children orally review the steps they had taken in preparing to listen?

8. What were Ms. Arnold's objectives? What did she hope students would learn?

9. Although this lesson is given at the beginning of the chapter on listening, in what respect is it a reading lesson?

10. In a Directed Listening Thinking Activity, students predict, listen with their predictions in mind, and clarify their predictions. In what way is this lesson a DLTA?

HENNINGS, *COMMUNICATION IN ACTION*

✳✳✳ Kinds of Listening ✳✳✳		
	Specific Listening Objectives	**Examples**
✳ **Informational**		
✳ **Critical-analytical**		
✳ **Critical-judgmental**		
✳ **Appreciative**		

HENNINGS, *COMMUNICATION IN ACTION*

Oral Communication:

Sharing Stories and Poems

Through Creative Activities

✳ ✳ ✳ *Higgledy, Piggledy* ✳ ✳ ✳

Higgledy, piggledy! See how they run!

Hopperty, popperty! What is the fun?

Has the sun or the moon tumbled into the sea?

What is the matter, now? Pray tell it to me!

Higgledy, piggledy! How can I tell?

Hopperty, popperty! Hark to the bell!

The cats and the mice even scamper away:

Who can say what may not happen today?

❄ ❄ ❄ The Animal Fair ❄ ❄ ❄

I went to the animal fair,

The birds and the beasts were there.

The big baboon by the light of the moon

Was combing his auburn hair.

The monkey he got drunk.

He stepped on the elephant's trunk.

The elephant sneezed

And fell to his knees,

And that was the end of the munk,
                    the munk,
                    the munk.

And that was the end of the munk.

HENNINGS, *COMMUNICATION IN ACTION*

Chapter 5, Master 4

✻ ✻ ✻ ✻ ✻ ✻ ✻ ✻ ✻ ✻ ✻ ✻ ✻ ✻ ✻ ✻ ✻ ✻

✻ ✻ ✻ MS. TOPPING'S LESSON ✻ ✻ ✻ DRAMA IN ACTION

✻ THE OBJECTIVES:

✻ WHAT TOPPING DID:	✻ WHY SHE DID WHAT SHE DID:

✻ YOUR REACTION TO THIS APPROACH—
PROBLEMS AND ADVANTAGES YOU SEE:

✻ OTHER CONTEXTS IN WHICH YOU COULD USE DRAMA:

✻ GENERALIZATIONS ABOUT DRAMA IN THE CLASSROOM:

HENNINGS, *COMMUNICATION IN ACTION*

✻ ✻ ✻ ✻ ✻ ✻ ✻ ✻ ✻ ✻ ✻ ✻ ✻ ✻ ✻ ✻ ✻ ✻

Oral Communication:

Sharing Ideas Through

Conversing and Reporting

✳✳✳✳✳✳✳✳✳✳✳✳✳✳✳✳✳✳✳✳✳✳✳✳✳✳✳✳✳✳✳✳✳✳✳

✳✳✳ MR. BRUCE'S LESSON ✳✳✳ AN IDEA FAIR

✳ The Objectives:

✳ What Bruce Did:	**✳ Why Bruce Did What He Did:**

✳ Your Reaction to This Approach—Problems and Advantages You See:

✳ Other Contexts in Which You Could Use the Idea Fair:

HENNINGS, *COMMUNICATION IN ACTION*

✳✳✳✳✳✳✳✳✳✳✳✳✳✳✳✳✳✳✳✳✳✳✳✳✳✳✳✳✳✳✳✳✳✳✳

➡ Question Writing Activity Guide ⬅

⇨ **Definitional   Questions:**

⇨ **Background   Information   Questions:**

⇨ **Hypothetical   Questions   Requiring   Projections
and   Guesses:**

⇨ **Relational   Questions:**

⇨ **Ethical   Questions:**

HENNINGS, *COMMUNICATION IN ACTION*

> **CONVERT THIS OUTLINE FIRST INTO A DATA CHART, THEN INTO A WEB. ASK: WHAT ARE THE ADVANTAGES OF EACH OF THESE GRAPHIC ORGANIZERS?**

🐻🐻🐻 Animals We Want to Meet 🐻🐻🐻

I. Koala
  A. Where it lives
    1. Kind of habitat
    2. Countries

  B. What it looks like (physical characteristics)

  C. What it does (behavioral characteristics)

II. Panda
  A. Where it lives
    1. Kind of habitat
    2. Countries

  B. What it looks like (physical characteristics)

  C. What it does (behavioral characteristics)

III. Kodiak bear
  A. Where it lives
    1. Kind of habitat
    2. Countries

  B. What it looks like (physical characteristics)

  C. What it does (behavioral characteristics)

HENNINGS, *COMMUNICATION IN ACTION*

Thinking Out Loud:

Talking, Listening, Writing,

and Reading Together

THE LORAX EPISODE I

1. **LIST THREE ASSUMPTIONS ABOUT LANGUAGE AND LANGUAGE LEARNING THAT INFLUENCE WHAT MR. DAG DOES IN HIS CLASSROOM.**

   •

   •

   •

2. **DRAW A SCHEMATIC OUTLINING MR. DAG'S LESSON.**

3. **EXPLAIN THE TEACHER'S FUNCTION IN THE LESSON.**

4. **DECIDE: OF THE TEACHING-IN-ACTION VIGNETTES YOU HAVE READ SO FAR, WHICH IS MOST SIMILAR TO THIS ONE? EXPLAIN YOUR REASONING.**

THE LORAX EPISODE II

5 GIVE THE REASON WHY MR. DAG USED THESE ACTIVITIES IN THE LESSON SEQUENCE:
A. THE FILM AT THE BEGINNING OF THE LESSON
B. THE SHOW OF HANDS TO INDICATE LIKING OR DISLIKING
C. THE CITING OF SPECIFIC EXAMPLES OF ACTS CHILDREN DISLIKED
D. CONSIDERATION OF WHOM THE ONCELER AND THE LORAX REPRESENT
E. RANK-ORDERING OF ACTS USING AN EVILS BOARD
F. COMPOSITION OF THE UNLESS PIECE AND THE ORIGINAL ALLEGORY
HENNINGS, *COMMUNICATION IN ACTION*

How does the teacher use it?

What is it?

What are the advantages?

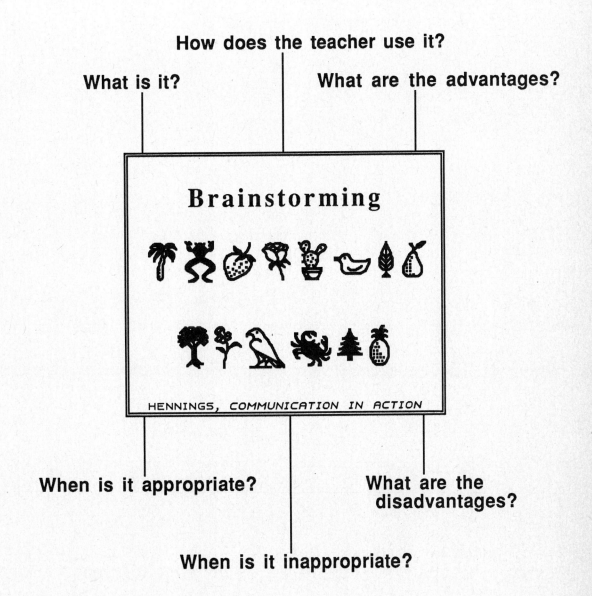

Brainstorming

HENNINGS, *COMMUNICATION IN ACTION*

When is it appropriate?

What are the disadvantages?

When is it inappropriate?

Writing as Idea Making: Thought in Action

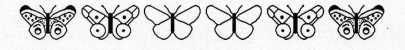

In Ms. Chou's Writing Classroom

Elements of The Lesson	Describe How She Handled That Phase of the Lesson	Tell Why She Did as She Did
Journal Writing		
Sharing of Writing		
Talking about Writing		
Modeling of Idea Making Through Mind Talk		
Modeling of Idea Making Through Idea Clustering		
Modeling of Writing Multiple Starts		

HENNINGS, *COMMUNICATION IN ACTION*

Working on Something in Process from Writing Folders		
Hearing and Talking about the Poem "Helping"		
Chorusing the Poem and Identifying Elements of Writing Style		
Brainstorming Writing Options Based on Reading		
Conferring		

HENNINGS, *COMMUNICATION IN ACTION*

✍ DIALOGUE JOURNALS ✍

HOW DOES THE TEACHER USE THIS FORM OF WRITING?

WHAT ARE THE ADVANTAGES OF DIALOGUE JOURNALS?

WHAT ARE THE DISADVANTAGES OF DIALOGUE JOURNALS?

The Writing Process

The Child Writer as Author

✳ Let's Make a Story from These ✳ Elements: A Guide for Rehearsing

Start by making a sentence that tells where the monster lived. Then tell what happened when he met the centipede. Use this guide to plot out your ideas before beginning to draft.

✳ Once upon a time

✳ Monster

✳ Hole

✳ Centipede

✳ Slipped

✳ Hollered

HENNINGS, *COMMUNICATION IN ACTION*

❋ Analysis Guide for Mr. Kamolsky's Lesson ❋		
Strategy	How He Used the Strategy	What He Was Trying to Achieve: His Objectives
Factstorming		
Categorizing and Charting		
Teacher-guided Group Writing		
Teacher-guided Group Editing		
Team Writing and Editing		
Revising/editing Workshop		

HENNINGS, *COMMUNICATION IN ACTION*

❀ ❀ ❀ The Writing Process ❀ ❀ ❀	
Aspects of the Process	**Ways to Organize in a Classroom**
❀ **Reading**	
❀ **Rehearsal**	
❀ **Drafting**	
❀ **Revision and Editing**	
❀ **Publication**	HENNINGS, *COMMUNICATION IN ACTION*

❀ ❀

✐ 📓 Analysis of Ms. Smith's Lesson 📓 ✐		
Strategy	**How She Used the Strategy**	**What She Was Trying to Achieve**
Story Reconstruction		
Choral Reading of Story		
Resetting of Punctuation		
Generalizing about Usage Patterns		
Applying the Generalizations by Resetting the Punctuation		
Writing Stories		

HENNINGS, *COMMUNICATION IN ACTION*

✏️ 📋 Analysis of Nouns and Verbs 📋 ✏️		
Kind of Proof	Noun	Verb

1. By meaning
 	
   Definition:
 	
   Example:		

2. By the way the
   word works
   in the sentence
   Definition:
 	
   Example:		

3. By the other
   words with
   which it patterns
   Definition:
 	
   Example:		

4. By inflectional
   endings
      Definition:
 	
   Example:		

5. By suffixes
      Definition:
 	
   Example:		

HENNINGS, *COMMUNICATION IN ACTION*

Spelling, Dictionary Use,

and Handwriting:

Tools of the Editor's Craft

STAGES IN SPELLING DEVELOPMENT

PRELITERATE SPELLING

AGE: CHARACTERISTICS:

LETTER NAME SPELLING

AGE: CHARACTERISTICS:

WITHIN-WORD PATTERN SPELLING

AGE: CHARACTERISTICS:

SYLLABLE JUNCTURE SPELLING

AGE: CHARACTERISTICS:

DERIVATIONAL SPELLING

AGE: CHARACTERISTICS:

HENNINGS, *COMMUNICATION IN ACTION*

Chapter 11, Master 3

∾ Mr. Bronsky's Spelling Lesson ∾		
Elements of the Lesson	Describe How He Handled That Element	Tell Why He Did What He Did
Sharing of Writing		
Talking about the Editing of Spelling		
Sorting Words		
Generalizing about Spelling		
Taking a Pretest		
Talking about How to Use the Dictionary		
Completing a Spelling Exercise		

HENNINGS, *COMMUNICATION IN ACTION*

∽∽ Looking at Handwriting Lessons ∽∽	
Activities	**Reason the Teacher Did What He/She Did**
∽ **How the Teacher Began**	
∽ **How the Teacher Developed the Skill**	
∽ **How the Teacher Refined the Skill**	HENNINGS, *COMMUNICATION IN ACTION*

Reading For Meaning:

Learning to Read and

Reading to Learn

Hennings, *Communication in Action*

▲ A Discussion Guide: ▲
▲ Inside Ms. Wilkening's Classroom ▲

1. How did Ms. Wilkening make words an integral part of her classroom?

2. How did Ms. Wilkening provide her children with prior experiences related to the story they would read together?

3. What levels of questions did Ms. Wilkening ask in relation to the story? In what ways did she develop her questions to help children comprehend the structure of the story?

Hennings, *Communication in Action*

4. Ms. Wilkening taught beginning decoding skills as an integral part of a meaningful lesson. How did she develop children's

▲ auditory discrimination skills?

▲ ability to read from left to right?

▲ sight word vocabulary?

▲ spelling skills?

▲ visual discrimination skills?

▲ sequencing skills?

5. How did Ms. Wilkening integrate reading, writing, and talking in her classroom? Do you think this is easy to do? Why? Why not?

6. Would you like to teach the way Ms. Wilkening does? Why? Why not?

Hennings, *Communication in Action*

Chapter 12, Master 3

Complete the data retrieval chart on teaching strategies by adding ideas from the text and ideas of your own.

✳ The strategy	✳ How to use the strategy	✳ What the strategy teaches
✳ Writing and reading stories in which a particular speech sound repeats		
✳ Masking words in a language experience chart or big book		
✳ Matching word cards to words in a language experience chart or big book		
✳ Joining in while listening to a repetitive story		
✳ Choral reading		
✳ Paired reading		
✳ Imitative reading		
✳ One-to-one reading		

Hennings, *Communication in Action*

✳✳ Teaching Strategies for Meaningful Reading ✳✳
✳ PREREADING STRATEGIES

✳ READING STRATEGIES

✳ AFTER READING STRATEGIES

HENNINGS, *COMMUNICATION IN ACTION*

✻✻ Specific Strategies for Teaching Reading ✻✻

✻ Think Alouds

✻ SQ3R

✻ Data Matrix

✻ Literature Group

✻ Reciprocal Questioning

✻ Guided Reading Procedure (GRP)

HENNINGS, *COMMUNICATION IN ACTION*

❑ A Guide for Analyzing a Basal Reading Series ❑

1. **Are there selections by respected writers? Give examples.**

2. **Is the distribution of story, poem, and informational selections suitable? Give examples.**

3. **Does the art complement the verbal aspects? Give examples.**

4. **How are the pupils' books organized? How do you react to that organization?**

5. **Are the selections such that the creative teacher can devise worthwhile and exciting ways to use them? Give examples.**

6. **How is the teacher's guide organized? How do you react to that organization?**

7. **Does the teacher's guide provide ideas for writing, listening, and speaking? Give examples.**

8. **Does the teacher's guide provide ideas for teaching comprehension strategies? Give examples. Can these be modified to meet individual needs? Give examples.**

HENNINGS, *COMMUNICATION IN ACTION*

☆ Significant Approaches ☆ ☆ to Reading Instruction ☆		
☆ **Approach**	**Major Philosophical Underpinnings**	**Critical Teaching Strategies**
Whole Language	Children learn to read by reading; they learn to write by writing. Children should be immersed in a world of print. Emphasis is on making meaning with print. Readers focus on the parts (sounds, letters) only when necessary to make meaning. Skills are taught through large units of instruction as part of content-area and literature encounters.	Predictable stories and big books for emergent reading; use of invented spelling; reading and writing across the curriculum; journal writing; focus units.
☆ **Approach**	**Major Philosophical Underpinnings**	**Critical Teaching Strategies**
Language Experience	Children learn to read by reading ideas most meaningful to them—selves—what they have experienced and written through dictation. The general sequence is from experience, to oral writing, to reading what one has written. Reading materials are created from class stories.	Language experience charts; individual dictation; first hand experiences; word, phrase, and sentence cards for use with experience story charts; phrase and sentence cards for reconstructing story charts. *Hennings Communication in Action*

☆ Significant Approaches ☆ ☆ to Reading Instruction ☆ ☆		
☆ **Approach**	**Major Philosophical Underpinnings**	**Critical Teaching Strategies**
Basal Reading	Children need considerable work with the skills of reading, especially with specific decoding and comprehension skills. Children need reading materials with carefully controlled vocabulary and readability at each grade level. Lessons should have considerable structure. Skills instruction should cycle from grade to grade.	Series of graded texts starting with readiness materials, preprimers, a primer, and readers for grades one through eight; ancillary materials that include teachers' manuals for each grade level, tests, instructional masters, workbooks, cards and charts, manipulatives, puppets, sometimes big books, kindergarten kits.
☆ **Approach**	**Major Philosophical Underpinnings**	**Critical Teaching Strategies**
Eclectic	There is no one right way to teach all children to read and write. Teachers must draw on all available resources and ideas, including whole language, language experience, and basal reading where appropriate.	Blend of strategies from all the other approaches. *Hennings, Communication in Action*

CHILDREN

WITH LANGUAGE

DIFFERENCES AND DIFFICULTIES

Hennings, *Communication in Action*

✛ With Ms. Venezia ✛		
Activity	**How She Used the Activity**	**Why She Used the Activity**
✛ **The Outing**		
✛ **Group Work for the Gifted**		
✛ **Group Work for the Language Slow**		
✛ **Group Work for the Language Different**		

Hennings, *Communication in Action*

✤ LANGUAGE ARTS FOR ALL CHILDREN ✤	
	KEY UNDERSTANDINGS
✤ BILINGUAL-BICULTURAL CHILDREN	
✤ DIALECTALLY DIFFERENT CHILDREN	
✤ SLOW LEARNERS	
✤ GIFTED AND TALENTED CHILDREN	
✤ CHILDREN WITH SENSORY IMPAIRMENTS	
✤ CHILDREN WITH SPEECH IMPAIRMENTS	Hennings, *Communication in Action*

TO INSTRUCTORS

We would like to respond to your instructional needs in future editions of
Communication in Action: Teaching the Language Arts. Your evaluation of this
edition will help us in that effort. Please complete the form below, and mail
it to Marketing Services; College Division; Houghton Mifflin Company; One
Beacon Street; Boston, MA 02108.

1. We would like to know your reaction to the following features of the text:

		Excellent	Good	Adequate	Poor
a.	Selection of topics	___	___	___	___
b.	Detail or depth of coverage	___	___	___	___
c.	Overall organization of the text	___	___	___	___
d.	Writing style/readability	___	___	___	___
e.	Value of the Teaching-in-Action descriptions that begin each chapter	___	___	___	___
f.	Value of the specific teaching ideas	___	___	___	___
g.	Value of the Forums and the descriptions of research studies in the text	___	___	___	___
h.	Value of the material given in the margin notes	___	___	___	___
i.	Value of the chapter summaries	___	___	___	___
j.	Value of the sections called Building and Refining Your Teaching Skills	___	___	___	___
k.	Student reaction to the text	___	___	___	___

2. We invite you to cite specific examples that illustrate any "adequate" or "poor" ratings.

3. Do you use the book as part of an undergraduate course?____graduate course?____workshop?____both undergraduate and graduate courses?____

4. What, in your opinion, is the strongest feature(s) of the book?

5. The weakest feature(s)?

6. How does our book compare with others that are available for the course?

Book Title   Comparison

a. _____   _____

   _____   _____

b. _____   _____

                                   _____

c. _____   _____

                                   _____

7. In terms of the following features of the instructor's guide:

   a. Did you use any of the ideas for structuring college-level sessions in the language arts? Yes___ No___ What was your reaction to these suggestions?

   b. Did you in any way model your course outline after the suggested syllabuses given at the end of the instructor's guide? Yes___ No___

   c. Did you in any way use the bibliographies included in the guide? Yes___ No___

   d. Did you in any way use the short essay questions or midterm and final exams given in the guide? Yes___ No___

   e. Did you in any way use the multiple-choice questions given? Yes___ No___

   f. We invite any explanations of the answers you have given about the instructor's guide and an overall evaluation of its usefulness.

8. Do you intend to use the text again?